THE GOSPEL ACCORDING TO

ST JOHN

T0382360

St John

THE REVISED VERSION

EDITED WITH INTRODUCTION AND NOTES
FOR THE USE OF SCHOOLS

BY

ARTHUR CARR, M.A.
VICAR OF ADDINGTON, SURREY
FORMERLY FELLOW OF ORIEL COLLEGE, OXFORD

CAMBRIDGE
AT THE UNIVERSITY PRESS
1905

I patient stated much of the Lord's life
Forgotten or misdelivered, and let it work:
Since much that at the first, in deed and word,
Lay simply and sufficiently exposed,
Had grown   .   .   .   .   .
Of new significance and fresh result;
What first were guessed as points, I now knew stars,
And named them in the Gospel I have writ.

BROWNING. *A Death in the Desert.*

ἀμέραι δ' ἐπίλοιποι
μάρτυρες σοφώτατοι. PINDAR.

PREFACE BY THE GENERAL EDITOR
FOR THE GOSPELS AND ACTS.

THE Revised Version has to some extent super-
seded the need of annotation on the Gospels
and Acts, so far as the meaning of words and phrases
is concerned. But the present Edition will, it is hoped,
serve a good purpose in drawing the attention of young
scholars to the importance of some of the changes
made in that Version.

Another aim is to present in a clear and intelligible
form the best and most approved results of recent
theological work on these books.

The General Editor takes this opportunity of noting
that, as in *The Cambridge Bible for Schools*, each writer
is responsible for the interpretation of particular passages, or for the opinion expressed on any point of
doctrine. His own part is that of careful supervision
and occasional suggestion.

ARTHUR CARR.

CAMBRIDGE
UNIVERSITY PRESS

University Printing House, Cambridge CB2 8BS, United Kingdom

Published in the United States of America by Cambridge University Press, New York

Cambridge University Press is part of the University of Cambridge.

It furthers the University's mission by disseminating knowledge in the pursuit of
education, learning and research at the highest international levels of excellence.

www.cambridge.org
Information on this title: www.cambridge.org/9781107651050

© Cambridge University Press 1905

First published 1905
First paperback edition 2014

A catalogue record for this publication is available from the British Library

ISBN 978-1-107-65105-0 Paperback

CONTENTS

		PAGE
INTRODUCTION	. . . .	ix—xxviii
I.	The Authorship of the Gospel . .	ix
II.	Life of St John	xv
III.	The Object and Characteristics of the Gospel	xviii
IV.	The Word or Logos	xxi
V.	The Discourses recorded by St John .	xxv
VI.	Analysis of the Gospel	xxviii
TEXT AND NOTES	. . . . . .	1—140
INDEX TO NOTES .	. . . . . .	141—144

MAPS

Palestine	. . . .	*Frontispiece*
District of Galilee	. . . . .	*After* p. 20

INTRODUCTION.

I. *The Authorship of the Gospel.*

THAT John the son of Zebedee was the author of the Gospel which bears his name has not been undisputed in recent times. But in an elementary work of this kind it will be sufficient to point out how strong the evidence of authenticity is, both from external sources, and from the Gospel itself; and hence the extreme improbability that the Fourth Gospel could have been composed later than the beginning of the second century, or by a writer unacquainted with Palestine in the time of our Lord.

The earliest direct statement as to the origin of the Gospel is found in the works of Irenæus (*c.* A.D. 185), a disciple of Polycarp, who was a contemporary and disciple of John himself. The two long lives of St John and Polycarp make a direct continuous link between the Ministry of Christ and the middle of the second century A.D. The words of Irenæus are to this effect[1]: 'I distinctly remember...what were the accounts he (Polycarp) had heard from them (the apostles) about the Lord, and about His miracles, and about His teaching; how Polycarp, as having received them from eyewitnesses of the life of the Word, used to give an account harmonizing on all points with the Scriptures." After recording the origin of the three synoptic Gospels Irenæus adds (*Hær.* III. i. 1):

[1] Lightfoot, *Biblical Essays*, p. 55, and Euseb. *H. E.* v. 20.

"John the disciple of the Lord, who had leaned his head on His breast, himself also published the Gospel while he dwelt at Ephesus in Asia." Clement of Alexandria (b. *circa* 150–160) who tells us that he had collected evidence from various Churches, and from the elders in his own Church, gives similar testimony: "John, the last of the Evangelists, having ascertained that the external (lit. 'bodily,' σωματικά) facts have been set forth in the Gospels, persuaded by men of repute and divinely moved by the Spirit, composed a spiritual gospel" (Eus. *H. E.* VI. 14).

It is impossible to believe that either Irenæus or Clement of Alexandria could have been deceived in so vital a matter, or that they would have ascribed to St John the Apostle a Gospel composed by some other writer at a much later date.

The testimony is much strengthened by the fact that the same belief prevailed in Churches so widely separated as those of Ephesus, the home of Polycarp, of Lyons, where Irenæus was Bishop, and of Alexandria, where Clement presided over the Catechetical School.

The evidence of these three fathers is confirmed by a valuable document known as the Muratorian Fragment, which internal proof shews to belong to the close of the second century A.D. This fragment apparently contained a list of the Canonical Books then recognised. The Fourth Gospel is there stated to have been written by St John at the request of his fellow disciples and bishops.

Apart from direct quotation the influence of this Gospel is discernible in the language and references of many heretical as well as Catholic writers in the second century[1]. Traces of the Gospel appear in the letters of St Ignatius, the Epistle of Barnabas, the *Didachè*, and *The Shepherd* of Hermas, none of which are probably later than 140 A.D.,

---

[1] Lightfoot's *Biblical Essays*, p. 90, note 3.

and since the publication of the Arabic version of Tatian's *Diatessaron* or Harmony of the Gospels in 1888, no doubt remains that the Fourth Gospel was known to this writer, who flourished about A.D. 155–170[1].

The only exception to this stream of ancient testimony is the assertion of the *Alogi*[2], an obscure heretical sect, that the Fourth Gospel was the work of Cerinthus. The grounds of the assertion are not difficult to explain or refute, and it is to be noted that although the authenticity of the Gospel is attacked, the date is not impugned, as Cerinthus was a contemporary of St John.

Moreover the Gospel was accepted as genuine by both sides in the ecclesiastical controversies which arose in the middle of the second century between Catholics and Montanists and in the Quartodeciman controversy. But if the Gospel had at that time recently seen the light, its authenticity would certainly have been fiercely disputed.

To this may be added the fact that Origen (b. A.D. 185), who wrote a commentary on the Gospel, gives no hint that its authenticity was doubted.

It is an interesting confirmation of this written testimony that in the Catacombs at Rome, before the end of the second century, there are found frequent representations of parables and events peculiar to St John's Gospel. Chief among these are 'the Good Shepherd,' 'the Vine,' 'the Woman of Samaria,' and 'the Raising of Lazarus[3].'

It may be noted in addition that so astonishing a literary fact as the production of the Fourth Gospel towards the end of the second century would not have passed without remark or observation by contemporary Christian writers. The author of such a work could not have passed

---

[1] *Studies in the Gospels*, by Vincent Rose, p. 15.

[2] The 'Unreasonable,' so named by Epiphanius. Lightfoot, *Biblical Essays*, p. 80.

[3] *Le Pitture delle catacombe Romane*, illustrate da Giuseppe Wilport. 1903.

into obscurity or have been confused with the Apostle St John immediately after the publication of his Gospel.

With this general consensus of external testimony the evidence drawn from the contents of the Gospel is in full agreement.

We have to shew that the Gospel was written by an eye-witness of the events which he records, consequently by a Jew living before the destruction of Jerusalem, by an Apostle of the Lord Jesus, and finally by St John.

The minute and exact knowledge of Jewish customs, names of places, social and political organization, religious sects, and the underlying Hebraisms of style, prove conclusively, because undesignedly, that the author of the Gospel was a Jew who was living in Palestine before the overthrow of the Jewish people by the Roman armies ; an event which produced so great a revolution in the condition of the country, and of the national life, that it would have been impossible for an alien living at a distance from Palestine, and in a later age, to reproduce with minute accuracy the state of things existing during our Lord's earthly Ministry.

In illustration of these points the following passages among many others may be cited. For names of obscure places, Chapters ii. 1, 11, iv. 46, xxi. 2 (Cana of Galilee, not mentioned in any earlier writer); i. 28 (Bethany beyond Jordan); xi. 54 (Ephraim, near to the wilderness); iii. 23 (Ænon, near to Salim); iv. 11 (Sychar, the city of Samaria, where Jacob's Well was). For Jewish customs and prevailing opinions : ii. 5, iii. 25, xi. 55, xviii. 28 (purification and ceremonial uncleanness); i. 28 (the meaning of baptism); ix. 2 (connexion between sin and suffering) ; vii. 35 (the disparagement of the 'Dispersion'); i. 21, iv. 25, vi. 14, vii. 40, xii. 34 (Messianic expectations). For social and religious conditions : iv. 27 (estimate of women); vii. 15 (rabbinical schools); iv. 9 (relation of Jews and Samaritans ; vii. 49 (contempt for the 'people of the earth').

But the internal evidence carries us farther than this. In three passages of this Gospel the writer of it affirms that he was himself a witness of that which he records. He witnessed the Christ Himself—the Incarnate Word, ch. i. 14. Compare with this 1 John i. 1. He witnessed at the Crucifixion the piercing of the Lord's side, and the issue therefrom of water and blood, ch. xix. 35. In ch. xxi. 24, after referring to himself as 'the disciple whom Jesus loved,' he adds, 'This is the disciple who witnesseth concerning these things and who wrote these things : and we know that his witness is true."

Here 'the disciple whom Jesus loved' is identified with the writer of the Gospel. But that St John the son of Zebedee was this beloved disciple admits of little or no doubt. For it will hardly be disputed that the disciple so honoured was one of those favoured three who, on several occasions, were chosen to be alone with Jesus. But that the writer of this Gospel was either St Peter or St James has never been suggested. It follows then that St John and the disciple whom Jesus loved are one and the same, and that he too is the writer of this Gospel.

Moreover, unless the beloved disciple was indeed John the son of Zebedee and the writer of the Gospel, we should be confronted with the fact that this leading Apostle, apart from his inclusion in the list of disciples ch. xxi. 2, is not once mentioned in the Fourth Gospel,—a supposition which is quite incredible.

Another indication that John the son of Zebedee was the writer of this Gospel is found in the fact that the Baptist is introduced into this Gospel as simply 'John' without any distinguishing title. The natural explanation of this is that John the Apostle being himself the writer there was no need of the distinctive title of the Baptist. But although this argument should have some weight, it cannot be pressed, since there are passages in the synoptic Gospels where John is mentioned without a descriptive title.

The same consensus of tradition which ascribes the authorship of the Gospel to St John, agrees that it was composed in the city of Ephesus at the close of the first or commencement of the second century. This belief is concisely stated in the passage from Irenæus cited above, and in the Muratorian Fragment.

Note. The tendency at the present time is not so much to deny the early date of the Gospel, as to deny the Apostolic authorship of it. Several modern critics ascribe the authorship to a certain presbyter John, who is named by Papias (Euseb. *H. E.* III. 39), as 'a disciple of the Lord.' It is however doubtful whether the presbyter John is not to be identified with the Apostle (see Blass, *Philology of the Gospels*, p. 222). And Zahn, with other leading German critics, "has thrown the weight of his massive learning on the side of the unqualified Apostolic genuineness of the Gospel." (*The Expository Times*, June 1900.)

Dr James Drummond, Principal of Manchester College, Oxford, in his work on the Character and Authorship of the Fourth Gospel arrives at the following conclusion:

"We have now gone carefully through the arguments against the reputed authorship of the Gospel, and on the whole have found them wanting. Several appear to be quite destitute of weight; others present some difficulty; one or two occasion real perplexity. But difficulties are not proofs, and we have always to consider whether greater difficulty is not involved in rejecting a proposition than in accepting it. This seems to me to be the case in the present instance. The external evidence (be it said with due respect for the Alogi) is all on one side, and for my part I cannot easily repel its force. A considerable mass of internal evidence is in harmony with the external. A number of the difficulties which have been pressed against the conclusion thus indicated melt away on nearer examination, and those which remain are not sufficient to weigh down the balance. In literary questions we cannot look for demonstration, and where opinion is so much divided we must feel some uncertainty in our conclusions; but on weighing the arguments for and against to the best of my power, I must give my own judgment in favour of the Johannine authorship."

On the question of authenticity Archbishop Benson wrote:

"I have no doubt that St John the Apostle wrote the Fourth Gospel, but if I thought some other had composed it, I should have one more surprising spiritual genius to admire with veneration, but it would not diminish the value of his Christ, of the Life and Light of the world." *Fishers of Men*, p. 89.

II. *Life of St John.*

St John[1] the Apostle, to whom the authorship of this Gospel is assigned on the above grounds, was the son of Zebedee and Salome and brother of St James, also an Apostle of our Lord. Of Zebedee nothing is known except that he was a fisherman on the Lake of Galilee, that he had hired servants, and that he was living at the time when his sons were called to the Apostleship. The most probable interpretation of John xix. 25, compared with Matt. xxvii. 56 and Mark xv. 40, indicates that Salome was a sister of Mary the mother of Jesus, and consequently her children James and John were first cousins of our Lord. St John is not once mentioned by name in this Gospel, but there can be little doubt that he is to be identified with the disciple of the Baptist who, when their master pointed to Jesus as the Lamb of God, followed Him (John i. 35–41). Note the significance of the words : 'He findeth first his *own* brother,' i.e. not the brother of his companion. A second call to the Apostleship is described in Matt. iv. 21, 22 ; Mark i. 19, 20 ; Luke v. 1–11. In the lists of the Apostles, St John is placed with his brother and Simon Peter and Andrew in the first group of four. St Mark tells us (iii. 17) that Jesus named the two sons of Zebedee *Boanerges*[2] or 'sons of thunder.'

[1] The name John (Johanan in the O.T.), was popularised in N.T. times as one of the Maccabean names, and became common, at any rate in a certain group. Three persons are mentioned in the Gospels bearing this name, John the Evangelist, John the Baptist, and John the father of Peter.

[2] It is not impossible that the name may date back to cousinly intercourse in childhood and have in it an element of humour or of affection. But as Mr Burkitt (cited in Wright's *Synopsis*) says, "No satisfactory explanation has been found for the word."

Whether the name refers to impetuosity of temper, or abruptness of speech, or to the Samaritan incident (Luke ix. 54), or to some other unrecorded passage in their lives is quite uncertain.

Characteristic notes of zeal come out in the incidents recorded in Luke ix. 54, where the sons of Zebedee desired to bid fire to come down from heaven on the Samaritans who would not receive Jesus; and in Mark ix. 38, where John forbids the man who, not being a follower of Jesus, cast out devils in His name. Their eagerness to be near Christ resulted in the claim, made through Salome, to sit on His right hand and on His left when He came in His Kingdom (Matt. xx. 20; comp. Mark x. 35).

On several occasions St John is specially chosen together with St Peter and St James to be with Jesus; at the raising of Jairus' daughter (Mk v. 37; Luke viii. 51); at the Transfiguration (Matt. xvii. 1; Mk ix. 2; Luke ix. 28); in the Garden of Gethsemane (Matt. xxvi. 36 and parallels). The same three, with the addition of St Andrew, seated on the Mount of Olives with Jesus enquire about the ultimate fulfilment of prophecy (Mk xiii. 3).

In the Fourth Gospel John is, as we have seen, 'the disciple whom Jesus loved.' As such he reclined on the *triclinium* next to Jesus (ch. xiii. 23 foll., where see notes). He was also probably the disciple mentioned as being 'known to the high priest' (ch. xviii. 16). It was to this disciple that Jesus tenderly committed the care of His mother (ch. xix. 26). To him and St Peter first is brought the news of the Resurrection (ch. xx. 2). And in ch. xxi. 'the sons of Zebedee' are thus named for the first time in this Gospel. They are standing with four other disciples on the shores of the Sea of Tiberias when Jesus appears to them. In answer to Peter's question, 'Lord, and what shall this man do?' Jesus says, 'If I will that he tarry till I come what is that to thee?'—a saying which gave rise to

the thought that John should not die. This erroneous
inference the Evangelist himself corrects (ch. xxi. 23).

Several traditions, some of great beauty, gathered
round the later years of St John's life. He appears to
have lived on in Jerusalem possibly until the destruction
of the city by Titus, and then to have retired to Ephesus,
which after the fall of Jerusalem became a great centre of
Christianity[1]. Possibly between the residence at Jerusalem and Ephesus St John visited Rome, where according
to an ancient legend he was placed in a caldron of boiling
oil and escaped unhurt. A trace of the former impetuosity
of temper appears in the story of his rushing from the
baths, which the heretic Cerinthus had entered, lest the
roof should fall. Still more characteristic were the stories
indicative of the Apostle's brave and loving spirit ; as
when he journeyed alone into the recesses of the forest in
order to reclaim a Christian youth who had joined a band
of robbers ; or as when in extreme old age he was carried
into the church and there again and again repeated the
words, "little children, love one another."

The date and circumstances of St John's exile in
Patmos are unknown. But the tradition is probable that
he was banished to that island under Domitian, and
released in the reign of Nerva.

There is no certain record of St John's death ; but the
prevalent belief is that he died peacefully at Ephesus
about the year 100 A.D. Irenæus, II. 22. 5, says he lived to
the age of Trajan, A.D. 98. The Chronicon Paschale states
that he survived to 104. Polycarp, the disciple of John,
was martyred 155 or 156. Irenæus was the disciple of
Polycarp.

---

[1] It was the home of St Andrew (Lightfoot, *Bib. Essays*, 52),
of Philip the Evangelist (Papias in Euseb. *H. E.* III. 39, Polycrates
in Euseb. III. 31, V. 24), perhaps also of Philip the Apostle
(Lightfoot, *Col.* p. 45), and of John the Presbyter, also a disciple
of Jesus. Others of the Apostles may also have resided there.

III. *The Object and Characteristics of the Gospel.*

The fact that the Gospel was written in the second or even the third generation after the death of Christ naturally gives a special character to this record as compared with the synoptic Gospels. Year by year the meaning of the life of Christ was more and more clearly revealed. Sayings and acts either unrecorded before, or recorded, but not fully understood, now stand forth full of significance in the light of history[1] : ' The days that follow after are the wisest witnesses[2].'

To this cause may be assigned the narratives of Nicodemus and of the Woman of Samaria, the fuller account of Feeding the Five Thousand, and the care with which the miracle of healing the man blind from his birth, or the raising of Lazarus, are narrated.

The object which St John had in writing the Gospel is distinctly stated in chapter xx. 31, "These are written that ye may believe that Jesus is the Christ, the Son of God, and that believing ye may have life in his name."

To this one object everything else is subordinated. To this, all incidents and sayings lead up. It is in this sense that St John's Gospel is called 'a spiritual gospel' by Irenæus. The facts are there, but the teaching and meaning and results of the facts are more important than the facts themselves. It is essentially a Gospel of faith ; a testimony to things unseen—a witness that things that are not seen are eternal.

---

[1] There are many instances in history of this later recognition of the relative importance of events. "The famous Parliament of Simon de Montfort in 1265 for instance is scarcely named by the contemporary historians, and only rises into importance as later history unfolds its real bearings." Bishop Stubbs, *The Early Plantagenets*, p. 32.

[2] ἁμέραι δ' ἐπίλοιποι
μάρτυρες σοφώτατοι. Pindar, *Ol.* I. 33.

But although with St John the external fact is of secondary importance, no Gospel is more vivid or even dramatic in its narrative parts.   Instead of merely stating opinions or conclusions, St John mixes as it were with the crowd and repeats what he hears this or that citizen saying to his neighbour (vii. 25, 40, foll.).   The scenes in which the first disciples are called stand out like pictures (i. 35, foll.),—the posture of the Baptist and his disciples, the sound of their footsteps, the look of Jesus, are carefully noted.   In all this description not a word is lost.   Each brings out some definite point   The tenses help to tell the story vividly and exactly.

Another notable feature of his Gospel is the accuracy with which points of time are mentioned.   See for example i. 39, iv. 6, 52, vii. 14, xix. 14.

The sense of the significance of all human action, but especially of the acts of Christ, is marked in this Gospel by the frequent use of the connecting particle 'therefore.' One event grows out of another as its cause, and so events take place on an ordered plan.   Closely connected with this thought is our Lord's declaration that His hour is not yet come (ii. 4, vii. 30, viii. 20), or that Jesus knew that His hour was come (xiii. 1).

A further characteristic of St John which appears in this Gospel is the Evangelist's grasp of character.   The portrait of St Peter would be incomplete without the descriptive touches in these chapters, especially perhaps in ch. xxi., where the interchange of words between Christ and His disciple is brought out with subtlety and exactness.   To St John we owe an insight into the beautiful spirit of Nathanael, the complex character of Nicodemus, and vivid traits in the portraits of St Thomas, Pilate, and Judas Iscariot.

But the most striking and valuable of all the attributes of St John is the deep spirituality, which enables him to discuss and indicate the hidden motives of our Lord's words and acts, and to present the revelation of the Son of God as no other of the Evangelists has done : see chs. ii. 24, vi. 6, 64, 71, vii. 39, viii. 27, xxi. 23. He speaks with authority as a prophet and interpreter of the mind of Christ. The words and thoughts of the Master have passed through the disciple's mind, and he records them in his own style and manner of writing. Without the Master, St John's words could not have been written ; but no one else could have reported our Lord's words as St John has reported them.

It has often been said that St John's Gospel is supplementary to the others. This is true. For not only does St John add many facts and sayings of our Lord unrecorded in the other Gospels, but he also corrects and enriches with supplementary details narratives common to him and the synoptists. To take one or two leading instances. Almost the whole of the Ministry in Jerusalem is peculiar to St John ; and the significance of the Feeding of the Five Thousand is enormously increased by the circumstances and results of that miracle recorded by St John alone. It is impossible to overestimate the spiritual value of his reminiscence of our Lord's words on the night of the Last Supper ; while the particulars added by this Evangelist in the narrative of the Passion are of surpassing interest and importance.

But it would be a mistake to regard the supplementary element as the chief or most important characteristic of this Gospel. St John's aim was, as we have seen, that his disciples should know 'him which is from the beginning' (1 John ii. 14 ; comp. John i. 1), and the portions of narrative or sayings of our Lord recorded by St John only, to the exclusion of others, are there, partly indeed because the other leading facts of the Gospel history were already known in the Church, but chiefly because these are the acts and sayings which seem to the Apostle most effectually to support his great thesis.

IV. *The Word or Logos.*

The Word or *Logos* holds so important a place in the teaching and theology of this Gospel that a fuller explanation of the expression must be given than is possible in a footnote.

From the way in which the conception is introduced in the Prologue to the Gospel it is clear that it must have been well understood by the disciples of St John, and also helpful to them in their understanding of the Gospel. The Preface or Prologue is not isolated. It must carry its meaning into the Gospel, which it introduces, and help to bring out the teaching of it.

It is true that the term *logos* had a place in the philosophical system of Philo (b. *circ.* 30 B.C.) and the Alexandrian school, and must have been well known at Ephesus in that connexion. But St John by his definition of 'the Word' dissociates his use of the term from that of Philo. The Word, whom St John identifies with the Christ of his Gospel, has no real connexion with the impersonal 'Word' of Philo. With St John the Word is a Person, and is God. With Philo the Word is an emanation and distinct from God[1].

And already, independently of Philo, 'the Word' was for the Jew a sacred name or title. Not only is there a near approach to personification of 'the Word' in the Psalms and in some passages of the Prophetical books, but the conception of Wisdom as delineated in such sublime chapters as Job xxviii. and Proverbs viii. is closely akin to 'the Word' of St John, and may even have in part suggested his phraseology.

[1] "There is a radical difference between the *Logos* of the Fourth Gospel, and the *Logos* of Philo...(the latter) is neither uncreated as God, nor created as man." Dr Edersheim, *sub voc.* Philo, *Dict. of Christian Biog.* "The logos of John and Ignatius is not the logos of Philo" (Harnack). See also *Logos* in Hastings' *Dict. of the Bible.*

But we may advance farther than this. For in the *Targums* or Chaldee paraphrase of the Old Testament Scriptures, *Memra* or 'Word' is substituted for Jehovah of the Hebrew original in many passages[1].

In his application of this term to the Christ then St John teaches two things :—(1) That he desires to connect the manifestation of the Christ with the conception of God in the Old Testament, and (2) that the term *Logos* or Word best explains this manifestation of the Christ, as the Revealer of God to man. Just as by speech as well as by act man is revealed to man, so Christ, the Word, in these two ways reveals the Father. This short preface then is closely connected with the whole of St John's teaching in this Gospel. It is the Gospel of the revelation of God in Christ. The keynote is to be found in the words of Philip to Nathanael (ch. i. 45), "We have found him, of whom Moses in the Law and the Prophets did write," i.e. whose character and work correspond to the highest attributes of God in the Law and the Prophets.

From this it appears that no one of the Gospels demonstrates the connexion between the theology of the Old Testament and the New Testament more clearly than this. The single sentence "My Father worketh hitherto, and I work," suffices to prove this continuity. And the first words of the Gospel indicate the meaning of it as a revelation carried on from the eternal past into the future. We are intended therefore to see in Christ the same character of the Godhead which is described in the Old Testament.

A few illustrations of this may be given. As God in Christ is revealed as a God of love in this Gospel, so in Hosea He is as a tender Father who taught

---

[1] Dr Edersheim gives a long list of these passages: *Jesus the Messiah*, II. p. 668. In the early chapters of Genesis alone the following texts are cited: Gen. ii. 8, iii. 8, 10, 24, iv. 26, v. 2, vii. 16, ix. 12, 13, 15, 16, 17, &c.

Ephraim to walk, holding him by his arms, who drew him to himself with human cords, with bands of love, Hos. xi. 1 foll.; see also Jer. xxxi. 3. Again in the Old Testament as in this Gospel God is a giver of life and of light; comp. Ps. xxxvi. 9 with St John i. 4, 5. See also Isai. xl. 6; xlix. 6; lii. 10; lx. 3 and Hosea vi. 5. The special message to Elijah was the sovereignty of God[1]; to Isaiah God is the God of righteousness, and of purity of worship; to the Psalmist He is shewn as One who knows the hearts of men; and to all the prophets He is the Redeemer of Israel and the God of unchanging constancy to His elect; and in all these ways Jesus Christ as the Word reveals God in this Gospel. The character of God appears in Him, He is the express image of God.

It is in accordance with this that St John sees in the miracles, signs or revelations of the Deity of Christ. In the earlier Gospels our Lord frequently enjoins those on whom He has wrought miracles 'to tell no man.' The miracle is wrought primarily for the benefit of the man himself, to confirm his faith, and to set him free from the bondage of sin. In this Gospel miracles are represented as wrought in order to shew that Jesus is the Messiah and that He is truly the Son of God. There is no injunction of silence. They are openly worked in the eyes of the people 'that the works of God should be made manifest,' ch. ix. 3, comp. ii. 11.

Another way in which Christ, as the Word of God, revealed the Father was His perfect conformity to the will of God. "I came not to do mine own will, but the will of him that sent me" (ch. vi. 38). So Jesus was the Apostle and Envoy of God. And just as a human envoy performs his office perfectly when he carries out his sovereign's will to the letter, and thus becomes his true representative, so Jesus Christ, the Apostle and Envoy of God, is His true

[1] R. Smith, *The Prophets of Israel*, p. 79.

and exact representative, for He is in fact Himself God, He is in unity with the Father: " I and the Father are one" (ch. x. 30). This is only in other words to say what St John had said before : "the Word was with God, and the Word was God " (i. 1).

It follows then that what makes the teaching about Jesus Christ in the Gospel according to St John specially suggestive and full of guidance for the religious life, is that it proves the whole of the Bible, and not the New Testament only, to be a revelation of Jesus Christ. St John by his description of Christ as the Word, takes his readers back to the contemplation of the character of God as it is revealed in the Old Testament, and at the same time leads them to think of the Christ as carrying on the ancient revelation to the clearer manifestation of the same God in the New Testament[1].

The Revelation of the Word.

A. *To the Responsive.* (a) To St John the Baptist and the first disciples: as the Creator of the world, the Life and Light of the world, the Incarnate Word, the Only-begotten from the Father (or, God Only-begotten), the Lamb of God, the Son of God, the Revealer of secrets.

(b) To His mother and His disciples : by the first sign in Cana of Galilee.

(c) To Nicodemus : by instruction, as the Revealer of mysteries, as the Son of God, the Son of Man, the Giver of Eternal Life, the Saviour.

(d) To the Woman of Samaria : by instruction, as a Prophet, as the promised Messiah.

(e) To Herod's courtier: by the second sign in Cana, as the Great Physician, as the hearer of prayer.

---

[1] Even in the Koran Jesus is spoken of as *The Word from God.*

B. *To the Irresponsive*: the Jews who rejected Him:
by signs and instruction, as the Lord of the Sabbath, as
the Beloved of the Father, as the Judge of the world, as
the predicted Messiah, as the Bread of Life, as the Giver
of the Spirit and the Giver of Life.

C. *To the Elect*, the inner circle of His disciples:
by discourses on humility, love, self-sacrifice, union with
Himself and one another, victory over the world.

V. *The Discourses recorded by St John.*

The discourses of Jesus recorded by St John differ in
form and motive from the synoptic reports. They are
such as came to be better understood and more enlightening as the Church advanced in experience. Again, they
deal with subjects requiring higher intelligence and more
thoughtfulness for their comprehension than could be found
among the unlettered crowds of Galilee.

Ch. iii. 1—15. **The discourse with Nicodemus.**
Here Jesus preaches the Gospel to a thoughtful scholar,
a Rabbi possessing authority as a member of the Sanhedrin. He first sweeps away the unspiritual Jewish conception of the kingdom ; then sets forth the meaning and
the necessity of the new birth. Only by water and the
Spirit, only by baptism (as men would clearly see afterwards), could any one enter the kingdom. Baptism is an
elementary, earthly truth. Beyond are deeper mysteries,
the Incarnation and the Atonement.

Ch. iv. 5—42. **The Woman of Samaria.** This discourse like the last contains a revelation of the spiritual
character of the kingdom of God. It is of supreme and
special interest, (1) as addressed to an alien, one outside
the Covenant, (2) as containing a declaration of Messiahship, (3) as predicting the cessation of the Temple-worship,

(4) as the self-revelation of the Prophet, who (*a*) penetrates the secrets of the heart, and (*b*) predicts the future, (5) as teaching the spiritual nature of true worship.

Ch. vi. 25—66. **The bread of life.** As the discourse with Nicodemus taught the truth about Baptism this discourse teaches the truth about the Eucharist. The three points which. make this conversation momentous in the history of doctrine are : (1) the teaching on the mode of the Atonement : (2) the teaching on the Eucharist in relation to the Atonement : (3) the statement of Election—the drawing of the Father—combined with human freedom.

The reference to the gift of manna is characteristic of the way in which the incidents of the Old Testament are cited in this Gospel : see ch. iii. 13, 14.

At the Feast of Tabernacles Jesus again delivers discourses of which, it would seem, fragments only are preserved, chs. vii., viii. In these the prevailing notes are (*a*) Christ's revelation of Himself to those who are in spiritual sympathy with the Father and with Him; and impossibility of revelation to those who do not know the Father. (*b*) A contrast between the external and earthly knowledge of Jesus and the deeper, spiritual knowledge of Him. (*c*) Christ the living Water:—the same figure as in ch. iv., but with changed circumstances and with special associations. (*d*) Christ the Light of the world. Again there is a twofold reference (1) to the ritual of the Feast, and (2) to the history of Israel, viii. 12. (*e*) The revelation of Himself in the Passion. (*f*) True freedom, and true sonship. A further teaching of the meaning of history.

Ch. x. 1—18. **Christ the Door of the fold. Christ the Good Shepherd.** This discourse springs from the circumstances of the preceding miracle. The immediate application is to the Pharisees and the priests, who are the robbers and the hirelings. Other inferences from the parable reach to the future of the Church. (1) The Oneness of the Church. One flock—One Shepherd—One Door. (2) The revelation of Christ to His own. The sheep know the voice of the Shepherd. (3) The expansion of the Church by the admission of the Gentiles as a result of the Atonement. (4) Sheep and pastor can enter by one way only, by Christ Himself.

Chs. xiii.—xvii. **The Discourses at the Last Supper.**
xiii. (1) Lessons of humility (12—20): (2) of love (31—35).
xiv. Comfort to the disciples in their Lord's departure. (1) The promise of heavenly rest. (2) The promise of the Comforter. (3) The promise of Christ's own presence. (4) The promise of peace.

Ch. xv. (1) The close and living union with Christ is illustrated by the similitude of the vine and its branches. (2) Love of the disciples to one another, and to the Father and the Son.

Ch. xvi. (1) The future of the Church—tribulation and the final reward. Sorrow *naturally* followed by gladness—a law of the Christian life. (2) The mission of Christ. (3) The confession of the Apostles. (4) The victory of Christ.

Ch. xvii. The intercessory prayer of the Christ—the great High Priest—for Himself, for His disciples, for His Church.

VI. *Analysis of the Gospel.*

Part I.   The Nativity and early Years.   i. 1—34.

    A. The Pre-existence of the Eternal Word, and His Incarnation, i. 1—14.

    B. The testimony of John the Baptist, i. 15—31.

    C. The Baptism of Jesus, i. 32—34.

Part II.   The Ministry, i. 35—xii. 50.

    A. Growth of the Gospel; partly in Galilee and Samaria ; partly in Jerusalem, i. 35—vii. 9.

    B. Conflict between belief and unbelief; wholly in Jerusalem, vii. 10—xii. 50.

Part III.   Passiontide, xiii.—xix.

    A. Intercourse with disciples—discourses at the Last Supper, xiii.—xvii.

    B. The Trials, Crucifixion, and Burial, xviii., xix.

Part IV.   The Resurrection, and post-Resurrection life, xx.

Part V.   Supplementary Chapter, xxi.

THE GOSPEL ACCORDING TO

ST JOHN.

PART I. The Nativity and Early Years.

I 1–34.

(a) The Prologue or Preface containing the revelation of the Eternal Word and of the Incarnation, 1–14.

IN the beginning was the Word, and the Word was 1 with God, and the Word was God. The same was in 2 the beginning with God. All things were made by him; 3

I. 1. In the beginning. The opening words recall, and are intended to recall, the first words of Genesis. This Gospel is the story of the new Creation. The **beginning** is the infinite past, inconceivable to human thought, and yet a necessary condition of thought, comp. 1 John ii. 13, 'ye know him which is from the beginning,' and Eph. i. 4, 'He chose us in him before the foundation of the world.'

the Word. See Introd., p. xxi. *foll.* St John's definition of this expression excludes the current philosophical meaning of it. Briefly stated, the meaning of 'the Word' is, God as revealed and revealing Himself to man. In the Liturgy of Sarapion God is addressed, 'Who through the Son was uttered and interpreted and made known to created nature.'

with God, the preposition 'with' ($\pi a\rho\acute{a}$), implies more than co-existence; it conveys the thought of intercommunion. See also 1 John i. 2.

3. All things were made by him. Revelation begins where science admits limitation. Sir O. Lodge says, 'Let us admit, as scientific men, that of real origin, even of the simplest thing, we know nothing, not even of a pebble.' And H. Spencer, 'The last conclusion of science is, a single unknown Cause, Power or Force manifested through all phenomena.' But Lord Kelvin notes that 'scientific thought is compelled to accept the idea of Creative Power.' With this comp. Hebr. xi. 3, 'By *faith* we understand that the worlds have been framed by the word ($\dot{\rho}\acute{\eta}\mu a\tau\iota$) of God.'

C.   I

and without him was not anything made that hath been
4 made. In him was life; and the life was the light of men.
5 And the light shineth in the darkness; and the darkness
6 apprehended it not. There came a man, sent from God,
7 whose name was John. The same came for witness, that
he might bear witness of the light, that all might believe
8 through him. He was not the light, but *came* that he

---

without him was not anything made. The Greek is
even stronger, 'not even one thing was made that hath been
made.' Comp. Heb. i. 2, 'His Son...through whom also he
made the worlds,' and Col. i. 16, 'In him were all things
created.' See the important marginal reading for the words
which follow: 'That which hath been made was life in him;
and the life' &c., which gives a true and profound meaning.

4. the life was the light of men. Light was the first
manifestation of the creative power of God, Gen. i. 3. 'It
is the indispensable condition of all order, all distinction, all life,
and all further progress' (Driver). This symbolism of God as
an O.T. thought is beautifully expressed in Ps. xxxvi. 9, 'With
thee is the fountain of life: and in thy light shall we see light.'
Comp. also Isaiah lx. 1, both passages regarded as Messianic in
Rabbinical writings. In the N.T. the figure is very frequent with
St Paul as with St John. The disciples of Christ are 'children
of the Light' (1 Thess. v. 5); their Master and Lord 'dwells in
light unapproachable' (1 Tim. vi. 16); and brought 'life and
incorruption to light' (2 Tim. i. 10). Scientifically too the
connexion between light and life is very close. 'The sun is the
source of all motion and force manifested in life on the earth'
(Asa Gray).

was the light. Note the tense. The light was obscured or
lost. It is a thing to be recovered through Christ, who is
our life.

5. apprehended it not, or overcame it not, *marg.* Either
rendering gives good sense. Either, (1) the world failed to
understand the Divine revelation, or, (2) in the conflict of light
and darkness, light was victorious.

6. There came, lit. was made. The use of the same verb as
in *v.* 3 marks a connexion between the creation of the world and
the coming of John. He too 'was made' and took his place in
the order of creation and in the Divine plan.

7. for witness. John, in whom the prophetic office was
revived, bore witness, (1) by prediction, and (2) by interpreting
Christ as the light and life of the world.

might bear witness of the light. There was the true light, 9
even the light which lighteth every man, coming into the
world. He was in the world, and the world was made by 10
him, and the world knew him not. He came unto his 11
own, and they that were his own received him not. But 12
as many as received him, to them gave he the right to
become children of God, *even* to them that believe on his
name: which were born, not of blood, nor of the will of 13
the flesh, nor of the will of man, but of God. And the 14
Word became flesh, and dwelt among us (and we beheld
his glory, glory as of the only begotten from the Father),
full of grace and truth.

---

9. coming into the world. The participle might agree
either with 'the true light,' or with 'every man.' The first
is preferable. There is a continuous infusion of the light of
the world. To each soul there is a possibility of enlightenment,
i.e. of life, see above *v.* 4.

With the thought of the continuous incoming of the Light of
the world we may connect the description of the baptized as
'enlightened,' and 'enlightenment' as a name for baptism.

10, 11. Neither the world which He created, nor the home
and the people whom He chose, recognised or welcomed the
Christ: 'They gave the Cross, when they owed the Throne'
(Browning).

12. as many as received him. The new Israel. Those who
through faith recognised and welcomed the Christ have the
privilege of sonship in Him. To become children of God
is more than to be children of Abraham.

13. The new life cannot be traced to any material cause, or
human impulse. It comes from God; and the condition of it is
faith in Him. In 1 John v. 18, 'Whosoever is begotten of God
sinneth not, but he that was begotten of God keepeth him.'

14. the Word became flesh, i.e. became man, was incarnate,
and so infused Divine life into human nature.

dwelt among us. Lit. tabernacled among us, i.e. either
(1) sojourned, or (2) dwelt among us in the tabernacle of His
flesh. Comp. 2 Cor. v. 4. Some have seen here an allusion to
the *Shekinah*, or manifestation of Jehovah's presence under the
Old Covenant, the Greek word for tent (*skenè*) being similar in
sound to *Shekinah*.

his glory, the manifestation of Himself as God. There may
be a special reference to the Transfiguration.

grace and truth. Grace in a special Christian sense is the

(*b*) John the Baptist testifies to Jesus as the Christ, 15-34,
(*a*) in his preaching, 15-18; (*b*) in answer to the priests
and Levites, 19-28; (*c*) in the presence of Jesus, 29-34.

15 John beareth witness of him, and crieth, saying, This was
he of whom I said, He that cometh after me is become
16 before me: for he was before me. For of his fulness we
17 all received, and grace for grace. For the law was given
18 by Moses; grace and truth came by Jesus Christ. No
man hath seen God at any time; the only begotten Son,
which is in the bosom of the Father, he hath declared
him.

19 And this is the witness of John, when the Jews sent

---

revelation of the Gospel as contrasted with the Law (see *v.* 16);
the gift of redemption in Christ, see Eph. i. 6, 'His grace which
he freely bestowed upon us in the Beloved.' As a trait of
character 'grace' is lovingkindness in imparting gifts, gracious-
ness in word and act. Comp. Ps. xxxvii. 21, R.V., and
Ps. xlv. 2; Is. lxi. 1-3. As a Greek word grace also signified
beauty and charm in speech and manner, see Pind. *Ol.* i. 30.

truth is conformity to reality in word and act, and to an ideal
perfection. Comp. 'truth as in Jesus,' as the norma and test
of all truth.

15. Comp. Matt. iii. 11.

16. of his fulness, with reference to 'full of grace and truth,'
v. 14. Comp. Eph. i. 23, 'the fulness of him that filleth all in
all,' and Eph. iii. 19, iv. 13; Col. i. 19, ii. 9. In these passages
'fulness' signifies the plenitude or sum total of Divine attributes
concentrated in God and in Christ.

we, the Apostles.

grace for grace, grace succeeding grace, lit. one grace taking
the place of another. Perhaps here the grace of the Gospel in
exchange for the grace of the Law.

17. grace and truth, see *v.* 14. Jesus Christ is here named
for the first time. The mystic and eternal Word is at last
revealed as Jesus Christ.

18. No man hath seen God. The connexion seems to be
that the unseen God is revealed in Christ as Father.

the only begotten Son. For this the remarkable reading,
'God only begotten,' is found in some leading MSS., and is
accepted by Westcott and Hort.

19. the witness of John. Here the Evangelist speaks from
his own experience as a disciple of the Baptist. **The Jews.**
St John always associates with this term hostility to Jesus. He

unto him from Jerusalem priests and Levites to ask him,
Who art thou? And he confessed, and denied not; and 20
he confessed, I am not the Christ. And they asked him, 21
What then? Art thou Elijah? And he saith, I am not.
Art thou the prophet? And he answered, No. They 22
said therefore unto him, Who art thou? that we may give
an answer to them that sent us. What sayest thou of
thyself? He said, I am the voice of one crying in the 23
wilderness, Make straight the way of the Lord, as said
Isaiah the prophet. And they had been sent from the 24
Pharisees. And they asked him, and said unto him, Why 25
then baptizest thou, if thou art not the Christ, neither

---

had lived to witness a national rejection of the Messiah by the
Jews. From *v.* 24 we learn that this mission consisted of
Pharisees.

20. the Christ, the expectation of the Messiah (Christ) had
grown in intensity as the political prospects of the nation
darkened. Vivid interest was excited by each claim to the
Messiahship.

21. Art thou Elijah? See Malachi iv. 5, and Matt. xvii. 11,
Mark ix. 13. The Baptist here shews that he was ignorant
of our Lord's interpretation of Malachi's prophecy (see Matt.
loc. cit.).

the prophet, see Deut. xviii. 15, 'The Lord thy God will raise
up unto thee a prophet from the midst of thee, of thy brethren,
like unto me, unto him shall ye hearken.' The expectation was of
some great lawgiver of a new Covenant; comp. Jer. xxxi. 31 f.,
see also *v.* 25 below and chs. vi. 14, vii. 40. The Christians
referred the prophecy to Christ Himself, Acts iii. 22.

23. the voice of one crying in the wilderness, &c., cited from
Isaiah xl. 3, there the voice of the herald announcing the
'gospel' or good tidings of deliverance from Babylon. This was
no unheeded voice as 'preaching in the wilderness' is often
interpreted to mean. 'There went out unto him Jerusalem and
all Judæa, and all the region round about Jordan,' Matt. iii. 5.

25. Why then baptizest thou? Although lustrations were
usual among the Jews, and baptism of the proselytes was
practised (Schürer, II. 11, 19), baptism of repentance for remission
of sins (Mark i. 4) was an innovation. As a sign or seal of
discipleship (Acts xix. 3) the Messiah (Ezek. xxxvi. 25;
Zech. xiii. 1) or Elijah or the Prophet might have enjoined it;
but what right had John to do this?

26 Elijah, neither the prophet? John answered them, saying, I baptize with water: in the midst of you standeth
27 one whom ye know not, *even* he that cometh after me,
   the latchet of whose shoe I am not worthy to unloose.
28 These things were done in Bethany beyond Jordan, where
   John was baptizing.

29   On the morrow he seeth Jesus coming unto him, and
   saith, Behold, the Lamb of God, which taketh away the
30 sin of the world! This is he of whom I said, After me
   cometh a man which is become before me: for he was
31 before me. And I knew him not; but that he should

---

26.   The answer of John is an assertion of his right to baptize
as a prophet of the greater One, still unrecognised, who was
coming after him.   It was a preparatory rite.

27.   the latchet of whose shoe, &c., the work of the meanest
slave.   Comp. Acts xiii. 25.

28.   Bethany, for Bethabara, A.V.   The site of this Bethany
beyond Jordan is quite uncertain.   It may be the Aramaic form
of the Hebrew Bashan, and denote that district.   Bethabara of
the A.V., meaning 'crossing' or 'ferry,' has been identified with
the modern Abârah, a ford 14 miles S. of the Sea of Galilee.
But such a name may have occurred more than once down the
river.   See G. A. Smith, *Hist. Geog. of the Holy Land*, p. 496.

29.   the Lamb of God.   The first reference is probably to the
lamb of the paschal sacrifice 'without blemish and without spot'
(1 Peter i. 19, 20—a passage which throws great light on this).
But the thought of 'the servant of the Lord,' led as a sheep to
the slaughter, must not be excluded, Is. liii. 7; comp. Acts viii.
32–36.   More generally the lamb is a symbol of innocence
and gentleness.   'A lamb is a sort of personified innocence by
reason of its whiteness, its meek expression, its pathetic voice.'
(C. Rossetti, *The Face of the Deep*, pp. 176, 177.)

The frequent use of this symbol of Christ in the Revelation is
to be noted (see chs. v. 5, xiii. 8, and elsewhere)—a sign of
the deep impression this word of the Baptist made on his
disciple, the Evangelist.

which taketh away the sin of the world, see 1 Peter i. 19.

30.   See *v.* 15.

31.   I knew him not, i.e. either (*a*) knew Him not as the
Messiah, or (*b*) literally; John brought up in the desert had
never seen Jesus.   He had no personal knowledge of Him.   And
yet even so the 'Holy Families' of the great medieval painters

be made manifest to Israel, for this cause came I baptizing
with water. And John bare witness, saying, I have beheld 32
the Spirit descending as a dove out of heaven; and it
abode upon him. And I knew him not: but he that 33
sent me to baptize with water, he said unto me, Upon
whomsoever thou shalt see the Spirit descending, and
abiding upon him, the same is he that baptizeth with the
Holy Spirit. And I have seen, and have borne witness 34
that this is the Son of God.

---

have a germ of truth. For, although the whole secret of the
Divine birth and the Messiahship of Jesus had not been revealed,
John knew enough of the wondrous and innocent childhood to
form a lofty conception of Jesus. Hence the words in Matt.
(iii. 14), 'I have need to be baptized of thee, and comest thou to
me?' Hence too his ready acceptance of the sign.

for this cause, &c., the end or first cause of John's baptism
was the revelation of Jesus as the Christ, made first to John and
through John to others.

32. The synoptics add the voice from heaven: 'Thou art my
beloved Son in whom I am well pleased,' Mark i. 11; Matt. iii.
17; Luke iii. 22: the two first apparently describe the vision as
witnessed by Jesus; St Luke notes that our Lord was *praying*
when the heavens were opened.

With the descent of the Spirit in the form of a dove at
this new creation compare 'the moving' (*Heb.* hovering as
of a bird) of the Spirit of God upon the face of the waters at the
first creation, Gen. i. 2.

abode, denoting the continual presence of the Holy Spirit on
Jesus. See Is. xi. 2, 'The spirit of the Lord shall *rest* upon
him.'

34. this is the Son of God, the definite conclusion of the
Baptist's testimony that Jesus the Christ is Divine. The expression 'Son of God' signifies identity of nature without any
notion of succession in time, or of inferiority.

It will be noted that the Baptist's testimony as reported in
this Gospel is more decisive as to the Divine nature (*v.* 34) and
office (*v.* 36) of Christ, than the synoptic report. Observe too
that St John does not record the act of baptism.

PART II.   The Ministry. I 35—II 55.

The first call of the disciples, 35—51. A valuable addition to the
    Synoptic account.   It describes the gradual inner drawing
    of the disciples with Jesus before they were summoned to
    be with Him.

35   Again on the morrow John was standing, and two of
36 his disciples; and he looked upon Jesus as he walked,
37 and saith, Behold, the Lamb of God! And the two
38 disciples heard him speak, and they followed Jesus. And
    Jesus turned, and beheld them following, and saith unto
    them, What seek ye? And they said unto him, Rabbi
    (which is to say, being interpreted, Master), where abidest
39 thou? He saith unto them, Come, and ye shall see.
    They came therefore and saw where he abode; and they
    abode with him that day: it was about the tenth hour.
40 One of the two that heard John *speak*, and followed him,
41 was Andrew, Simon Peter's brother. He findeth first
    his own brother Simon, and saith unto him, We have
    found the Messiah (which is, being interpreted, Christ).

---

35.   John was standing.   In A.V. less accurately 'stood.'
He was standing to continue his work of baptizing.

two of his disciples.   Andrew, see *v.* 40, and probably
the Evangelist himself.   This is inferred from the minute details
of his testimony, and from his usage of silence in respect to
himself.

36.   looked upon Jesus.   The Greek word implies an earnest,
penetrating look, lit. 'looking in him': the same word is used *v.* 42.

37.   followed Jesus, a result of the preparatory work of the
Baptist.

38.   being interpreted, Master.   This note shews that St John
wrote for Greek readers.

39.   the tenth hour, 4 o'clock p.m. if the reckoning was from
6 a.m. as usual.   This is one of the many points of precise
accuracy in statement which distinguishes this Gospel.

40.   Simon Peter's brother.   This description of Andrew
shews that, when St John wrote, St Peter was better known in
the Church than St Andrew.

41.   He findeth first his own brother Simon.   There can
be little doubt that this implies that afterwards he finds his
companion's brother, James, the son of Zebedee.

We have found the Messiah.   This 'finding' implies search.

He brought him unto Jesus. Jesus looked upon him, and 42
said, Thou art Simon the son of John : thou shalt be
called Cephas (which is by interpretation, Peter).

On the morrow he was minded to go forth into Galilee, 43
and he findeth Philip : and Jesus saith unto him, Follow
me. Now Philip was from Bethsaida, of the city of 44
Andrew and Peter. Philip findeth Nathanael, and saith 45
unto him, We have found him, of whom Moses in the law,
and the prophets, did write, Jesus of Nazareth, the son of
Joseph. And Nathanael said unto him, Can any good 46
thing come out of Nazareth? Philip saith unto him, Come
and see. Jesus saw Nathanael coming to him, and saith 47
of him, Behold, an Israelite indeed, in whom is no guile !

They were fellow students of Scripture, as were Philip and
Nathanael (*v.* 45).

42. son of John, by far the best supported reading, replacing
'son of Jona,' A.V.

Cephas. The Aramaic form of the Hebr. *Ceph* a rock.
The new name signified a fresh departure in life and work ; or a
changed condition. Comp. Is. lxii. 2, 'Thou shalt be called by
a new name, which the mouth of the Lord shall name.'

These four, the first called, form a group by themselves and
are always placed at the head of the list of the Twelve. This is
the germ of an organized Church. Special capacity destined
these four for a special place in the ministry.

43. On the morrow, the second day of the ministry of Jesus.

Philip is the first disciple whom Jesus Himself finds ; comp.
ch. ix. 35. The name is Greek and indicates the Graeco-
Macedonian influence. For other notices of Philip see chs. vi.
5-9, xii. 21, 22, xiv. 8, 9.

44. Bethsaida. See Map.

45. Nathanael. Most probably to be identified with Bartholomew. Nathanael seems to rank as an Apostle here and in
ch. xxi. 2. But his name does not appear in the synoptic lists ;
on the other hand Bartholomew is not named in the Fourth
Gospel. If the two are identified all difficulty vanishes.

From this address it appears that Philip and Nathanael were
friends and fellow students of the Law and the Prophets. Philip
comes to the conclusion affirmed by Christ Himself, Luke xxiv.
26, 27.

46. Nathanael's objection seems formidable, but is solved by
the presence of Jesus.

48 Nathanael saith unto him, Whence knowest thou me?
Jesus answered and said unto him, Before Philip called
thee, when thou wast under the fig tree, I saw thee.
49 Nathanael answered him, Rabbi, thou art the Son of God;
50 thou art King of Israel. Jesus answered and said unto
him, Because I said unto thee, I saw thee underneath the
fig tree, believest thou? thou shalt see greater things
51 than these. And he saith unto him, Verily, verily, I say
unto you, Ye shall see the heaven opened, and the angels
of God ascending and descending upon the Son of man.

2 1-11. The marriage feast in Cana of Galilee. The first
miracle of Jesus.

2   And the third day there was a marriage in Cana of
2 Galilee; and the mother of Jesus was there: and Jesus

---

48. when thou wast under the fig tree, probably engaged
in prayer or confession, or in meditation on the coming of the
Messiah; and that in a spot inaccessible to any human eye.
For this manifestation of Christ as knowing the secret thoughts
and lives of men see ch. iv. 16, 17, and comp. Ps. cxxxix. 1-3.
The well-known incident of St Augustine's conversion took
place under a fig-tree: *Confessions*, VIII. 12-28.

51. Verily, verily. This repeated affirmation is peculiar to
this Gospel.

the angels of God ascending and descending. The reference
is undoubtedly to Gen. xxviii. 12.

The angels ascending and descending denote uninterrupted
spiritual communication between the Christ and God. For
Jacob the vision was an assurance of Divine protection: Jesus by
recalling the vision indicated that He, the Son of man, has at
command the forces of heaven which ascend and descend to do
His bidding. Christ is Son of man as well as Son of God (*v.* 49).
He is the representative man, the second Adam, in Whom all
are made alive, in Whom all humanity is centred.

II. 1. the third day, probably the third day after leaving the
Jordan.

Cana of Galilee, so called to distinguish it from a Cana of
Cœle-Syria (Jos. *Ant.* xv. 5. 1). The site is disputed. The
existing Kâna el Jelîl, 6 miles N. of Nazareth, answers the
conditions, as an exact equivalent in name, as being above
Capernaum and on the way to Nazareth from the Jordan valley.

also was bidden, and his disciples, to the marriage. And 3 when the wine failed, the mother of Jesus saith unto him, They have no wine. And Jesus saith unto her, Woman, 4 what have I to do with thee? mine hour is not yet come. His mother saith unto the servants, Whatsoever he saith 5 unto you, do it. Now there were six waterpots of stone 6 set there after the Jews' manner of purifying, containing two or three firkins apiece. Jesus saith unto them, Fill 7 the waterpots with water. And they filled them up to the brim. And he saith unto them, Draw out now, and 8 bear unto the ruler of the feast. And they bare it. And 9 when the ruler of the feast tasted the water now become

---

The rival and traditional site is Kefr Kenna to the N.E. of Nazareth.

2. his disciples, the five or perhaps six, whose call has been described. It is often inferred that Jesus and His disciples had not been invited, but arrived as unexpected guests.

4. Woman. This mode of address implies no discourtesy or lack of respect. It is used with the utmost tenderness in the word from the Cross, ch. xix. 26.

what have I to do with thee? Again there is none of the abruptness in the original which appears in the English form. But no doubt the words mark a point of departure in the relations between mother and Son. Even He must leave mother and home and sisters for the sake of the Gospel. The work of the Redeemer of Israel is subject to no human control. Each act of the ministry has its appointed **hour**. See chs. vii. 30, viii. 20, xii. 23, xiii. 1, xvi. 21; also comp. Luke xxii. 53.

6. after the Jews' manner of purifying. Comp. Mark vii. 4; Hebr. vi. 2. Purification both of persons and of utensils and dishes was, and still is, religiously observed by the Jews, and it entered largely into the Pharisaic system.

firkins, from Old Dutch *vier*, four, with suffix *-kin*, the fourth part of a barrel, a measure equal to 9 gals.

8. Draw out now. It is not clear whether the direction was to draw from the water-pots or from the well. Probably the former. The servants were directed to draw the water, now made into wine, from the large water-pot with jugs or cans, from which it was poured into the drinking-vessels of the guests. (Field.)

9. the ruler of the feast. This would probably be one of the guests chosen for the purpose, the *arbiter bibendi*.

It is noted as an evidence of accuracy in detail that no ' friends

wine, and knew not whence it was (but the servants which
had drawn the water knew), the ruler of the feast calleth
10 the bridegroom, and saith unto him, Every man setteth
on first the good wine; and when *men* have drunk freely,
then that which is worse: thou hast kept the good wine
11 until now.   This beginning of his signs did Jesus in Cana
of Galilee, and manifested his glory; and his disciples
believed on him.

12. Jesus goes to Capernaum.

12   After this he went down to Capernaum, he, and his
mother, and *his* brethren, and his disciples: and there
they abode not many days.

13-25. In Jerusalem at the Passover.   The Cleansing of the
Temple.

13   And the passover of the Jews was at hand, and Jesus

---

of the bridegroom' are named in this narrative.   This custom
prevalent in other parts of Palestine did not exist in Galilee.
(Edersheim, *Life*, &c. I. p. 355.)
   10. setteth on first the good wine.   Here the A.V. 'doth
set forth,' is preferable, as the wine was not 'set on' the table
as with us, but poured into each cup as described above.
   11. signs, the term invariably used for miracles in this
Gospel and always so rendered in R.V.   They are visible proofs
of a hidden, Divine power.   In illustration of this see Mark ii. 9,
where the external result is used as a proof of the secret process
of forgiveness.   Miracles are also 'signs' as being acted parables.
Here for instance the good wine set forth last is used to symbolize
the Gospel dispensation.
   manifested his glory.   See i. 14; proved infallibly His Divine
power.   For His disciples it was an effectual sign.   They believed.   They were able to respond to the meaning of it.   The
effect on others is not named.   His 'brethren,' who were
probably at the feast (see *v.* 12), we know did not believe.
   12. Capernaum.   See Map.   The site is disputed; the question being between the modern Khân Minyeh and Tell Hum.
On the whole the latter is the more probable identification.
   there they abode, perhaps with relations.
   13. the passover of the Jews was at hand.   This is important as one of the few notes of time given in the Gospel.

went up to Jerusalem. And he found in the temple those 14
that sold oxen and sheep and doves, and the changers of
money sitting: and he made a scourge of cords, and cast 15
all out of the temple, both the sheep and the oxen; and
he poured out the changers' money, and overthrew their
tables; and to them that sold the doves he said, Take 16
these things hence; make not my Father's house a house
of merchandise. His disciples remembered that it was 17
written, The zeal of thine house shall eat me up. The 18
Jews therefore answered and said unto him, What sign
shewest thou unto us, seeing that thou doest these things?
Jesus answered and said unto them, Destroy this temple, 19

---

14. A similar act is recorded as taking place at the end of
the Ministry. There is no inherent improbability in this. And
indeed our Lord's object in purging the Temple seems to have
differed on the two occasions. The setting in each case is
distinct and appropriate. St John's accuracy in definition of
time is so marked that in this Gospel at any rate the incident
cannot be misplaced.

in the temple, i.e. in the Court of the Gentiles, the
outermost Court of the Temple. The oxen, sheep and doves
were sold for sacrificial purposes. It would be a convenience to
purchasers to have animals for sale which had been inspected
and passed as fit for sacrifice. The bankers, or money-changers,
were there to exchange foreign money for Jewish coins, with
which alone the Temple tribute and other offerings could be
paid. This Temple traffic was a source of great profit to the
priests, especially to the family of Annas (Edersheim, *Life*, &c.
I. 372). The absence of any resistance to 'the cleansing of
the temple' arose from the popular dislike to these 'bazaars,'
which were suppressed not long afterwards.

15. **cast all out of the temple, both the sheep and the
oxen.** Better perhaps, 'cast out all' (i.e. the dealers, &c.) and
the sheep and the oxen.

16. **make not**, &c. Comp. Zech. xiv. 21, 'There shall be no
more a trafficker in the house of the Lord of Hosts.'

17. See Ps. lxix. 9.

19. **Destroy this temple**, &c. The Evangelist explains this,
saying in a note *v.* 21, 'He spake of the temple (or sanctuary) of
his body.' Thus explained the prediction was verified by the
Resurrection. In another sense also it proved true. In succession

20 and in three days I will raise it up. The Jews therefore
   said, Forty and six years was this temple in building, and
21 wilt thou raise it up in three days? But he spake of the
22 temple of his body. When therefore he was raised from
   the dead, his disciples remembered that he spake this;
   and they believed the scripture, and the word which
   Jesus had said.

23   Now when he was in Jerusalem at the passover, during
   the feast, many believed on his name, beholding his signs
24 which he did. But Jesus did not trust himself unto them,
25 for that he knew all men, and because he needed not that
   any one should bear witness concerning man; for he himself knew what was in man.

3 1–21. The interview with Nicodemus.

3   Now there was a man of the Pharisees, named Nico-
2 demus, a ruler of the Jews: the same came unto him

---

to the Temple of the Jews destroyed by Titus rose the far more
glorious Temple of the Church of Christ. See Mk xiv. 58, where
the addition occurs, 'made without hands.'
   20. Forty and six years, &c. This was the Temple which
Herod the Great began to restore in B.C. 20 (Joseph, *B. J.* 1. 21).
It was not completed till A.D. 64.
   22. they believed the scripture, as for instance Ps. xvi. 10.
Comp. Acts ii. 24–28; Is. liii.; Acts viii. 32, 33, and the sign of
the prophet Jonah, Matt. xii. 39.
   For such later recognition of the meaning of the Lord's words,
which at first were not understood, see ch. xii. 16.
   23. at the passover. See above, *v.* 13.
   25. knew what was in man. Note this as a Divine attribute
in Christ.   Comp. Ps. cxxxix. 1, 'Thou understandest my
thought afar off'; Acts i. 24, and Rom. viii. 27.

   III. 1. a man, an instance of a man whose inmost thoughts
Jesus knew. See above, ch. ii. 25.
   a ruler of the Jews, i.e. a member of the Sanhedrin or
Supreme Council.

by night, and said to him, Rabbi, we know that thou art
a teacher come from God: for no man can do these signs
that thou doest, except God be with him. Jesus answered 3
and said unto him, Verily, verily, I say unto thee, Except
a man be born anew, he cannot see the kingdom of God.
Nicodemus saith unto him, How can a man be born when 4
he is old? can he enter a second time into his mother's
womb, and be born? Jesus answered, Verily, verily, I say 5
unto thee, Except a man be born of water and the Spirit,
he cannot enter into the kingdom of God. That which 6
is born of the flesh is flesh; and that which is born of the
Spirit is spirit. Marvel not that I said unto thee, Ye 7

---

2. by night, either from a fear of being compromised; or, in
order not to give Jesus the sanction of his authority by visiting
Him openly in the day. Comp. xix. 39, where this incident is
mentioned by way of contrast with the more courageous conduct
of Nicodemus afterwards.

Rabbi, i.e. Master, or great one, a term of deep respect,
especially as applied to one not educated in the Rabbinical
schools.

3. Except a man, &c. This great truth is revealed not in
answer to any word of Nicodemus, but to some thought of his
heart. Nicodemus seems to have expected instruction on the
old lines. Jesus teaches that a new birth and new spiritual
powers are needed for the kingdom of God. 'If any man is in
Christ, he is a new creature,' 2 Cor. v. 17.   **he cannot see.**
Only the new-born or spiritual can perceive the things that are
spiritual, and they who are like God will see Him. See 1 Cor.
ii. 11, 12, and 1 John iii. 2. It is difficult to decide whether
anew ('again,' A.V.) or 'from above,' *marg.*, is the better
rendering.

4. How can a man, &c. The objection of Nicodemus was a
serious one. Our Lord's words seemed to contradict the laws of
nature.

5. of water and the Spirit. A further explanation to which
the institution and practice of baptism for two generations had
given its full significance. The thought of baptism by immersion
adds vividness to the figure.

6. That which is born, &c. A clear revelation of two
co-existent lives beginning respectively with the natural birth
and the spiritual birth.

7. Marvel not, &c., because it is a law of nature that like
produces like.

8 must be born anew. The wind bloweth where it listeth,
and thou hearest the voice thereof, but knowest not
whence it cometh, and whither it goeth: so is every one
9 that is born of the Spirit. Nicodemus answered and said
10 unto him, How can these things be? Jesus answered and
said unto him, Art thou the teacher of Israel, and under-
11 standest not these things? Verily, verily, I say unto thee,
We speak that we do know, and bear witness of that we
12 have seen; and ye receive not our witness. If I told you
earthly things, and ye believe not, how shall ye believe,
13 if I tell you heavenly things? And no man hath ascended
into heaven, but he that descended out of heaven, *even*
14 the Son of man, which is in heaven. And as Moses lifted

---

8. The wind bloweth, or, 'The spirit breatheth,' *marg.*
Both in Hebrew and in Greek the same word is used for 'wind'
and 'spirit.' The wind is indeed the best possible symbol of the
Spirit. Each, itself invisible, is recognised by results.

10. the teacher, for 'a teacher,' A.V. The definite article
points to Nicodemus as a representative of the Rabbinical
schools.

11. We speak that we do know. The evidence of spiritual
truth is direct and intuitive, and is beyond the region of
argument.

12. earthly things, i.e. spiritual truths concerning things
transacted here and under the conditions of this life, as opposed
to the yet unrevealed mysteries of Heaven. Comp. 2 Esdras
iv. 11, 'How can he that is already worn out with the corrupted
world understand incorruption?' See also *vv.* 10 and 21 of the
same chapter.

13-15. These sayings could only be understood when the
facts had taken place to which they allude. It is another
instance of this Evangelist's retrospective teaching, i.e. shewing
the meaning of our Lord's words in the light of history.

the Son of man. As the Son of God is the express image of
God, one with Him in nature and essence, so the Son of man is
the express image and type of perfect manhood; and in Himself
sums up all humanity. With the exception of St Stephen
(Acts vii. 56), and St James (Euseb. *H. E.* ii. 23), the title is
used exclusively by Jesus of Himself. The absence of the title
in Christian literature is remarkable, and may be accounted for
by the fear of a misconception in its meaning, as if it were 'Son
of a man.' The origin of the name may perhaps be traced to

up the serpent in the wilderness, even so must the Son of man be lifted up: that whosoever believeth may in him 15 have eternal life.

For God so loved the world, that he gave his only 16 begotten Son, that whosoever believeth on him should not perish, but have eternal life. For God sent not the 17 Son into the world to judge the world; but that the world should be saved through him. He that believeth on him 18 is not judged: he that believeth not hath been judged already, because he hath not believed on the name of the only begotten Son of God. And this· is the judgement, 19 that the light is come into the world, and men loved the darkness rather than the light; for their works were evil. For every one that doeth ill hateth the light, and cometh 20 not to the light, lest his works should be reproved. But 21

Dan. vii. 13, 14 (see *Studies in the Gospels*, by V. Rose, p. 158 foll.). In the Book of Enoch it is used as a Messianic title. In Ezekiel it occurs frequently, but there in reference to the weakness of the prophet as man.

14. See Numb. xxi. 9. This saying gives our Lord's authority for the typical interpretation of Holy Scripture.

15. whosoever believeth may in him, &c., for 'whosoever believeth in him' &c., *marg.* and A.V. This important change is justified by the reading of the best MSS. (ἐν for εἰς).

16-21. A note by the Evangelist to explain the last saying of Jesus, and to shew the result of His Death and Resurrection. Others however attribute the words to Christ Himself. If so, the words are not a survey of the work of Christ in the world, but a prediction by Christ of His own Divine purpose, and of the nature of the kingdom. The former view is the more probable, and more in accordance with the method of the Evangelist. The cause and motive of the Atonement are stated. The motive is the love of God; the final cause, eternal life.

17. sent with a definite mission, as an Apostle. **to judge**, for 'to condemn,' A.V.

18. believed on the name, &c., i.e. belief on the Son of God as manifested in the Gospel, and expressed by baptism into the name of Jesus Christ, Acts ii. 38.

19. In rejecting the light men pass judgment on themselves.

he that doeth the truth cometh to the light, that his works
may be made manifest, that they have been wrought in
God.

22-36 and 4 1-3. Jesus in Judæa baptizing; John also baptizing.

22 After these things came Jesus and his disciples into
the land of Judæa; and there he tarried with them, and
23 baptized. And John also was baptizing in Ænon near to
Salim, because there was much water there: and they
24 came, and were baptized. For John was not yet cast into
25 prison. There arose therefore a questioning on the part
26 of John's disciples with a Jew about purifying. And they
came unto John, and said to him, Rabbi, he that was with

---

21. doeth the truth, for 'doeth truth,' A.V. 'Every fragment of truth done is so much light made visible' (Bp Westcott).

22. baptized. In this Gospel only is baptism by Jesus (or
His disciples, ch. iv. 1) named.

23. The exact position of Ænon, and of Salim, the more
important place, is unknown. Col. Conder however has
pointed out Ainûn in the Wady Fâr'ah as a probable identification. Here are rock-cut cisterns and a succession of springs
answering to the 'many waters' of the Greek. See R.V. *margin.*
Salim, east of Shechem, is 7 miles from Ainûn.

24. John was not yet cast into prison. A knowledge of
the Baptist's history is taken for granted by this Evangelist.
The prison was probably at Machærus, a fortress and palace of
Herod Antipas on the eastern cliffs of the Dead Sea. See
Matt. iv. 12; Mark i. 14; Luke iii. 20.

25. therefore, in consequence of the different baptisms by
Jesus and by John, and their disciples. The Baptist himself
distinguished his own baptism from the baptism of Christ,
Matt. iii. 11.

a questioning, or discussion, better than 'a question,' A.V.
Note **a Jew** for 'the Jews,' A.V.   **about purifying,** see
Hebr. vi. 2, where teaching about 'baptisms' is named among
the elementary points of Christian instruction; comp. also
Mark vii. 4.

26. There is a certain tone of resentment, and jealousy for
their master's honour, in this question of the disciples, which
throws into greater prominence the truthfulness and moral
courage of the Baptist's reply. The temptation to self-exaltation
is absolutely rejected.

thee beyond Jordan, to whom thou hast borne witness,
behold, the same baptizeth, and all men come to him.
John answered and said, A man can receive nothing, 27
except it have been given him from heaven. Ye your- 28
selves bear me witness, that I said, I am not the Christ,
but, that I am sent before him. He that hath the bride 29
is the bridegroom: but the friend of the bridegroom,
which standeth and heareth him, rejoiceth greatly because
of the bridegroom's voice: this my joy therefore is fulfilled.
He must increase, but I must decrease.   30

He that cometh from above is above all: he that is 31
of the earth is of the earth, and of the earth he speaketh:
he that cometh from heaven is above all. What he hath 32
seen and heard, of that he beareth witness; and no man
receiveth his witness. He that hath received his witness 33

---

27. Comp. James i. 17, 'Every good gift and every perfect
boon is from above, coming down from the Father of lights.'

29. Here the figure of Christ as bridegroom is used to express
His higher relation in regard to John. The bride may be
regarded as the new Israel, the Church, of which Christ is
Lord. For the custom from which the illustration is drawn see
Edersheim (*Jewish Social Life*, p. 153 foll.), who shews that our
Lord's words are in harmony with the locality in which they
were spoken.

30. **I must decrease.** To human eyes John's mission
seemed to be a failure. Once all Jerusalem went out to hear
him; in the end he was cast into prison, and his work ceased.

31-36. A note of the Evangelist on the Baptist's words.
Christian experience has proved the truth of this witness of the
Baptist to Christ. Christ the heavenly Teacher is above all
earthly teachers in being from heaven (31), in testifying what
He has seen (32).

32. **beareth witness...receiveth.** Observe the present tenses;
Christ is still testifying and man still refusing to receive His
testimony. It is a note of the small response to the Gospel
when St John wrote.

33. **He that hath received his witness.** The ultimate appeal
in matters of faith is to the Christian consciousness, to the soul
which responds to the truth about Christ. Comp. 1 Cor.
iii. 10 foll.

34 hath set his seal to *this*, that God is true. For he whom
God hath sent speaketh the words of God: for he giveth
35 not the Spirit by measure. The Father loveth the Son,
36 and hath given all things into his hand. He that believeth
on the Son hath eternal life; but he that obeyeth not the
Son shall not see life, but the wrath of God abideth on
him.

4 When therefore the Lord knew how that the Pharisees
had heard that Jesus was making and baptizing more
2 disciples than John (although Jesus himself baptized not,
3 but his disciples), he left Judæa, and departed again into
Galilee.

4-42. Jesus, passing through Samaria into Galilee, talks with
a woman of Samaria at Jacob's well.

4,5 And he must needs pass through Samaria. So he

---

set his seal to this (for ' hath set to his seal,' A.V.) confirms
the testimony by his own inner experience of the truth of God.
34. he giveth not the Spirit by measure, for ' *God* giveth,'
&c., A.V. The subject is not expressed in the Greek; and it
may be 'Christ,' in which case the meaning would be: 'As a
proof that Christ speaketh the words of God, He giveth not the
Spirit by measure.'
35. hath given all things into his hand. For this eternal
authority of Christ see Matt. xi. 27, xxviii. 18; Eph. i. 10;
Col. i. 16, 17.
36. obeyeth not, 'believeth not,' A.V. and R.V. *marg.*
the wrath of God is the judgment of God, which a man
brings upon himself by rejecting the light. See Rom. i. 18;
1 Thes. i. 10.

**IV. 1. Jesus was making and baptizing more disciples than
John.** This knowledge, as Jesus knew, would inflame the hatred
of His enemies, therefore He retired from Judæa. For the
moment He saved His life; but He saved it for the Cross. It
was no cowardly shrinking from danger. For another instance
of such retirement see Matt. xv. 21; Mark vii. 24.
2. This baptism by the disciples of Jesus was not the perfected
Christian baptism, but prepared the way for it. It was a baptism
of discipleship.
4. Samaria. Here the population was a mixed race descended from the Israelites, who had been left in the land when

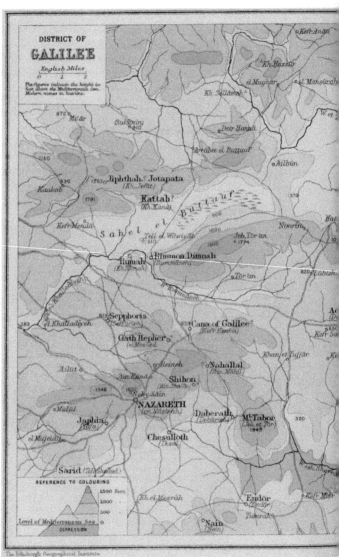

DISTRICT OF
GALILEE

English Miles
0   1   2

The figures indicate the height in
feet above the Mediterranean Sea.
Modern names in hair-line.

Kefr Anan

Kh. Hazur

el Mughâr   el Mansûrah

Kh. Sallâmeh

872 Ma'ar   Sukhnin   Deir Hannâ
           910

Arrâbet el Buttauf

Ailbûn

1160

330   1763   Jiphthah? Jotapata
Kaukab   (Kh. Jefât)
                                    379
       1791   Kattah?
              (Kh. Kana)   B u t t a u f

Kefr Menda   S a h e l   e l   508

                    Tell el Wawiyât   1090   Jeb. Tôr'an
                          510   6 1734
                                        1000
                                                            10
              Rumah   Rimmon Dimnah
              (Kh. Rumah) (Rummaneh)
                                     Tôr'an
                                                    820 Lûbieh
                              El Khamâneh

                                                    Ac
                                                    (P.
       el Khalladiyeh   813 Sepphoris   839 Cana of Galilee?
389   (Seffurieh)   (Kefr Kenna)   565 Kefr Sa

                    Gath Hepher
                    (el Meshed)

                         esh Sleineh   Nahallal
Ailut   Ain Runâs   (Ain Mâhil)
              1546   1607 Shihon   Khan et Tujjar
              Malûl   Ain Sa'in Ain Shaîn   Ke
                         NAZARETH
              Japhia   (en Nâsireh)   Daberath   Mt Tabor
              (Yâfa)   (Deburieh)   (Jeb. et Tôr)   320
el Mejeidil   1843
                    Chesulloth
                    (Iksâl)

       Sarid (Tell Shadud)   Besh Sheikh

REFERENCE TO COLOURING
                    1500 Feet
                    1000   Kh. el Mesrah   Endôr
                    500   (Endôr)   Kefr Mis
Level of Mediterranean Sea 0   Tamrah
       DEPRESSION   Nain
                                          (Nein)

The Edinburgh Geographical Institute

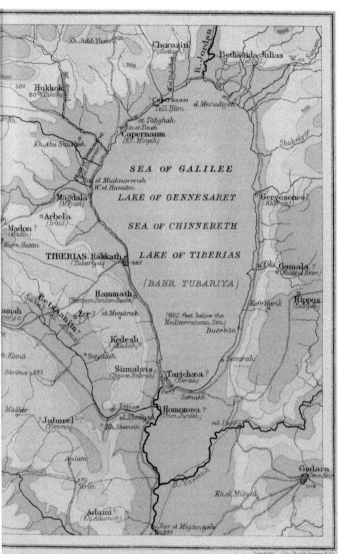

cometh to a city of Samaria, called Sychar, near to the
parcel of ground that Jacob gave to his son Joseph: and 6
Jacob's well was there. Jesus therefore, being wearied
with his journey, sat thus by the well. It was about the
sixth hour. There cometh a woman of Samaria to draw 7
water: Jesus saith unto her, Give me to drink. For his 8
disciples were gone away into the city to buy food. The 9
Samaritan woman therefore saith unto him, How is it
that thou, being a Jew, askest drink of me, which am
a Samaritan woman? (For Jews have no dealings with
Samaritans.) Jesus answered and said unto her, If thou 10
knewest the gift of God, and who it is that saith to thee,
Give me to drink; thou wouldest have asked of him, and
he would have given thee living water. The woman saith 11

---

the leading men were carried into captivity (B.C. 722), and the
foreign settlers imported by Esarhaddon (B.C. 701) to repeople
the land. Their hostility to the Jews (see *v.* 9) dated from the
days of Zerubbabel and Jeshua, when the Samaritans were not
allowed to share in the work of rebuilding the Temple. See
Ezra iv. 2 foll. The mission to Samaria was the first step in
the evangelization of the world (Acts i. 8).

5. Sychar, not to be confused with Shechem—an error
dating from the time of Jerome. An early traveller mentions a
Sichar E. of Shechem; and the name survives in a ruined hamlet
now called Askar. Jacob's Well still exists; its present depth is
about 75 ft. Water is only occasionally found in it. As there
are streams in the neighbourhood it is a matter of surprise that
the well should have been dug, or that the woman should have
come to it for water: but other instances are cited where people
will go to fetch water from a favourite well though a nearer
supply exists.

6. thus, *marg.* 'as he was,' i.e. without deliberate thought
or intention. Comp. Mark iv. 36 and the Lat. *sic temere,* Hor.
Od. II. xi. 14.

7. to draw water, not, as in patriarchal times, the work of
high-born women. She was therefore a poor woman.

8. the city, either Sychar, or Shechem, now Nablûs, a con-
traction of Neapolis (*νέα πόλις* or new city).

10. the gift of God, explained in the words that follow, the
living water, or Christ Himself, the gift of the Father, ch. ii. 6.

unto him, Sir, thou hast nothing to draw with, and the
well is deep: from whence then hast thou that living
12 water? Art thou greater than our father Jacob, which
gave us the well, and drank thereof himself, and his sons,
13 and his cattle? Jesus answered and said unto her, Every
14 one that drinketh of this water shall thirst again: but
whosoever drinketh of the water that I shall give him
shall never thirst; but the water that I shall give him
shall become in him a well of water springing up unto
15 eternal life. The woman saith unto him, Sir, give me
this water, that I thirst not, neither come all the way
16 hither to draw. Jesus saith unto her, Go, call thy
17 husband, and come hither. The woman answered and
said unto him, I have no husband. Jesus saith unto her,
18 Thou saidst well, I have no husband: for thou hast had
five husbands; and he whom thou now hast is not thy
19 husband: this hast thou said truly. The woman saith

---

11. **the well**, lit. the pit. (φρέαρ), a different word from the
well or fountain (πηγή) of *vv.* 6 and 14. See R.V. *marg.*, *v.* 6.

14. The pure, life-giving spring of water is a natural and
beautiful symbol of the Divine life recognised in the O.T.:
'Thou shalt make them drink of the river of thy pleasure. For
with thee is the well of life,' Ps. xxxvi. 8, 9. 'In that day there
shall be a fountain opened...for sin and for uncleanness,' Zech.
xiii. 1. With Jeremiah the Lord is 'the fountain of living
waters,' ii. 13, xvii. 13.

the water that I shall give him. Note the contrasts in this
parable of Jacob's Well. For the living water there is no long
way to come (*v.* 15); the very fountain of life is *here* (*v.* 26); no
painful drawing ('the well is deep'); He will *give* (*v.* 10); no
after-thirst (*v.* 13), 'Whosoever drinketh of the water that I shall
give him shall never thirst.'

15. **neither come all the way hither.** The addition of the
R.V. 'all the way' is due to a change of reading in the Greek.
But even with the change of reading the change of rendering is
hardly needed.

16, 17. The Christ reveals Himself in many ways. Here by
a way which the woman would clearly understand, and which
touches her conscience. Comp. ch. i. 43, where also Christ
reveals Himself as one who knows the secrets of a man's life.
See Ps. cxxxix. 1–3.

unto him, Sir, I perceive that thou art a prophet. Our 20
fathers worshipped in this mountain; and ye say, that in
Jerusalem is the place where men ought to worship.
Jesus saith unto her, Woman, believe me, the hour 21
cometh, when neither in this mountain, nor in Jerusalem,
shall ye worship the Father. Ye worship that which ye 22
know not: we worship that which we know: for salvation
is from the Jews. But the hour cometh, and now is, 23
when the true worshippers shall worship the Father in
spirit and truth: for such doth the Father seek to be his
worshippers. God is a Spirit: and they that worship 24
him must worship in spirit and truth. The woman saith 25
unto him, I know that Messiah cometh (which is called
Christ): when he is come, he will declare unto us all

---

20. The use which the woman makes of her recognition of
Jesus as a prophet and revealer of her secret life is remarkable.
She makes no confession, but instantly refers to him for solution the great dispute between Jew and Samaritan. Instead of
being drawn into argument, Jesus, after vindicating the Jewish
position in the dispute (*v.* 22), reveals the great truth, that
henceforth religion shall not depend on local or material conditions, neither on mountain nor temple. It shall be spiritual and
world-wide. This was indeed the teaching of the O.T., which
predicts a universal religion; see 1 Kings viii. 27 and 2 Chron.
ii. 6. Christianity realises it; Judaism has remained 'national
and particularist.' It is this argument which underlies St
Stephen's speech (Acts vii., see esp. *v.* 48) and inspired St Paul.
See Rom. iii. 29, xv. 9.

21. this mountain, Gerizim, which stands on the south side
of the valley, facing Mt Ebal on the north. See Deut. xxvii.
12 foll.

24. God is a Spirit, &c., i.e. unlimited by time or space, or
any material attribute. Worship must be spiritual. Its sphere
is the spiritual part of a man, which is akin to the Divine nature.
in truth. Worship in truth has been made possible by the
revelation of God in Christ, who is the truth. The soul that
knows Christ perfectly worships God in truth.

25. I know that Messiah cometh. Possibly the whole
conversation and something in the presence of Jesus suggested
the thought of the Messiah rather than the immediately preceding
words.

he will declare unto us all things. This was her simple

26 things. Jesus saith unto her, I that speak unto thee am
   he.
27   And upon this came his disciples; and they marvelled
   that he was speaking with a woman; yet no man said,
   What seekest thou? or, Why speakest thou with her?
28 So the woman left her waterpot, and went away into the
29 city, and saith to the men, Come, see a man, which told
   me all things that *ever* I did: can this be the Christ?
30
31 They went out of the city, and were coming to him. In
   the mean while the disciples prayed him, saying, Rabbi,
32 eat. But he said unto them, I have meat to eat that ye
33 know not. The disciples therefore said one to another,
34 Hath any man brought him *aught* to eat? Jesus saith
   unto them, My meat is to do the will of him that sent me,

Messianic expectation. The Christ would be a Divine teacher
and a revealer of the secrets of the heart. See *v.* 29.
   26. I that speak unto thee am he. This self-revelation of
Himself to the Samaritan woman contrasts with the usual reticence of Jesus in this respect even with His own disciples.
   27. marvelled that he was speaking with a woman, for
'that he talked with the woman,' A.V., a slight but important
correction both in the tense, and in the change to the indefinite
article. The marvel was that He was speaking with a woman
at all. The rabbinical rules as to this were very stringent, e.g.
'Let no man speak with a woman in the street, even though she
be his wife.' The restraint therefore of the disciples in questioning their Master is a sign of the great awe in which they held
Him. Comp. ch. xxi. 12.
   28. left her waterpot, either because she intended to return,
or from forgetfulness of all else in her great news. She became
an Evangelist of a simple Gospel to her fellow-countrymen.
   29. Her conception of the Christ as a revealer (*v.* 25) is
made personal: 'who told *me* all things that *I* did.'
   can this be, for 'is not this,' A.V.
   32. I have meat to eat that ye know not. The thought
left in the Saviour's mind from the interview was that suggested
in *v.* 21, the mission of the kingdom.
   33. For this literalness on the part of the disciples see
Matt. xvi. 6 and parallels.
   34. to do the will of him that sent me. Comp. Matt.
xxvi. 42.

and to accomplish his work. Say not ye, There are yet 35
four months, and *then* cometh the harvest? behold, I say
unto you, Lift up your eyes, and look on the fields, that
they are white already unto harvest. He that reapeth 36
receiveth wages, and gathereth fruit unto life eternal;
that he that soweth and he that reapeth may rejoice together. For herein is the saying true, One soweth, and 37
another reapeth. I sent you to reap that whereon ye have 38
not laboured: others have laboured, and ye are entered
into their labour.

And from that city many of the Samaritans believed 39
on him because of the word of the woman, who testified,
He told me all things that *ever* I did. So when the 40
Samaritans came unto him, they besought him to abide
with them: and he abode there two days. And many 41
more believed because of his word; and they said to the 42
woman, Now we believe, not because of thy speaking:

---

that sent me. Jesus was an Apostle of the Father. See
ch. xvii. 18.
to accomplish his work. Compare with this the words from
the Cross: 'It is finished,' ch. xix. 30.
35. There are yet four months, &c. This may be a note of
time, or merely a proverbial expression. In any case the com-
parison has a local significance. The vast expanse of growing
corn visible at this spot is far from a common sight in Palestine.
No doubt the crowd of Samaritans descending from Sychar
suggested the thought of the spiritual ingathering in the near
future.
36. He that reapeth. The marginal reading is to be pre-
ferred: 'Already he that reapeth receiveth wages.' The spiritual
harvest has so quickly ripened in Samaria that Jesus (He that
soweth) and His disciples (he that reapeth) may rejoice together.
That talk with the woman was a sowing, the fruits of which the
disciples were even now reaping. But the words of Christ had
a wider meaning in the success of the Apostles' mission work
prepared for by the work of Christ.
40. they besought him to abide. A wonderful concession
in face of the bitter hostility between Jew and Samaritan.
Probably no Jew had accepted hospitality from a Samaritan
for centuries—ever since the days of Ezra and Nehemiah.

for we have heard for ourselves, and know that this is indeed the Saviour of the world.

43-45. The reception of Jesus in Galilee.

43 And after the two days he went forth thence into
44 Galilee. For Jesus himself testified, that a prophet hath
45 no honour in his own country. So when he came into Galilee, the Galilæans received him, having seen all the things that he did in Jerusalem at the feast: for they also went unto the feast.

46-54. Cure of the nobleman's son in Galilee.

46 He came therefore again unto Cana of Galilee, where he made the water wine. And there was a certain noble-
47 man, whose son was sick at Capernaum. When he heard

---

42. the Saviour of the world. A marked advance in the conception of the Messiah. Personal intercourse with Jesus taught the Samaritans that He was more than a teacher or revealer of secrets, as the woman had announced.

The conversion of the Samaritans was the beginning of the Church of the Gentiles; and the breaking down of the barriers of race hatred. It was the first visible success of the Ministry of Jesus. The sight of the citizens of Sychar streaming down the mountain side was a sign and foreshadowing of that great harvest which is still unreaped.

44. For...his own country, i.e. Judæa. A contrast with Galilee is suggested by the context. And undoubtedly Judæa was the native land of the Saviour born in Bethlehem. Moreover the Jews of Jerusalem had markedly rejected Jesus: 'He came unto his own and they that were his own received him not,' ch. i. 11. Any other interpretation of 'his own country' presents great difficulties. How for instance can 'for' be explained if Galilee is intended by 'his own country'? And to interpret Galilee of one part of Galilee as distinct from another is forced and unnatural.

46. a certain nobleman, or, 'king's officer' (*marg.*). He was probably one of the officials at the court of Herod Antipas, and as such may have heard of Jesus from John the Baptist. He would certainly have been known to Joanna, wife of Chuza, Herod's steward (Luke viii. 3), and to Manaen, the foster-brother of Herod. The former may have been ministering to Jesus at this very time. It is possible that the boy may have seen Jesus, and that it was at his request that the father sought Him.

that Jesus was come out of Judæa into Galilee, he went
unto him, and besought *him* that he would come down,
and heal his son; for he was at the point of death. Jesus 48
therefore said unto him, Except ye see signs and wonders,
ye will in no wise believe. The nobleman saith unto him, 49
Sir, come down ere my child die. Jesus saith unto him, 50
Go thy way; thy son liveth. The man believed the word
that Jesus spake unto him, and he went his way. And as 51
he was now going down, his servants met him, saying,
that his son lived. So he inquired of them the hour when 52
he began to amend. They said therefore unto him,
Yesterday at the seventh hour the fever left him. So the 53
father knew that *it was* at that hour in which Jesus said
unto him, Thy son liveth: and himself believed, and his
whole house. This is again the second sign that Jesus 54
did, having come out of Judæa into Galilee.

5 1–14. Cure of the sick man at the pool of Bethesda.

After these things there was a feast of the Jews; and **5**
Jesus went up to Jerusalem.

---

48. Except ye see signs and wonders, &c. The verb is in
the plural. The words are addressed to the Galileans generally,
not specially to this man. Without signs and wonders His
message would be ignored.

49. The courtier makes no reply, only persists in prayer.
His faith however is less perfect than that of the centurion
(Matt. viii. 8), who could say, ' only say the word and my servant
shall be healed.'

52. Yesterday. It must be remembered that the Jewish day
began at sunset, so that it is not necessary to suppose that a
night had intervened.

V. 1. a feast of the Jews. *Marg.* 'the feast.' If 'the feast'
be read it might mean the Feast of Tabernacles. But that feast
would probably have been named as it is ch. vii. 1. This
remark also applies to the Feast of the Passover (ii. 13, vi. 4,
xi. 55), and of the Dedication (x. 22), which are named. The
Feast of Purim in March would agree best with iv. 35, but
there is nothing in the context which points to that season.
Pentecost would not leave a long enough interval for the events

2 Now there is in Jerusalem by the sheep *gate* a pool,
which is called in Hebrew Bethesda, having five porches.
3 In these lay a multitude of them that were sick, blind, halt,
5 withered. And a certain man was there, which had been
6 thirty and eight years in his infirmity. When Jesus saw
him lying, and knew that he had been now a long time *in
that case*, he said unto him, Wouldest thou be made whole?
7 The sick man answered him, Sir, I have no man, when
the water is troubled, to put me into the pool: but while
8 I am coming, another steppeth down before me. Jesus
9 saith unto him, Arise, take up thy bed, and walk. And
straightway the man was made whole, and took up his
bed and walked.
10 Now it was the sabbath on that day. So the Jews said

---

from the Passover of ch. iii. 13. On the whole the Feast of
Trumpets at the beginning of the new (civil) year in September
seems most probable.

2. sheep gate (not 'sheep market' A.V.), probably on the
east side of Jerusalem, the side on which lay the vast pasture
lands of Judæa. Its identification with the modern St Stephen's
gate is doubtful.

Bethesda. 'Some ancient authorities read Bethsaida or
Bethzatha' *marg.* The derivation of Bethesda is uncertain
and its situation unknown. Possibly it was the intermittent
spring in the Upper Pool, known as the Fountain of the Virgin.
This uncertainty is itself a proof of the authenticity of the Gospel:
'What forger would have ventured to introduce or localise so
obscure and contested a spot?' (Cp. Lightfoot, *Bib. Essays.*)

4. A verse omitted here in R.V. and also by the leading
editors, embodies a popular tradition that 'an angel went down
at a certain season into the pool and troubled the water; whosoever then first after the troubling of the water stepped in was
made whole of whatsoever disease he had.'

5. thirty and eight years, the duration of the infirmity is
named partly to shew the wonder of the cure, partly as a special
cause for the compassion of Jesus: see next verse.

7. The sick man for 'The impotent man' A.V.

8. take up thy bed, that is the mat on which the Orientals
sleep, and which can be easily carried.

9. it was the sabbath on that day. See ch. ix. 14, and
Matt. xii. 10 foll.

unto him that was cured, It is the sabbath, and it is not lawful for thee to take up thy bed. But he answered 11 them, He that made me whole, the same said unto me, Take up thy bed, and walk. They asked him, Who is 12 the man that said unto thee, Take up *thy bed*, and walk? But he that was healed wist not who it was: for Jesus 13 had conveyed himself away, a multitude being in the place. Afterward Jesus findeth him in the temple, and 14 said unto him, Behold, thou art made whole: sin no more, lest a worse thing befall thee.

15–18. The question of work done on the sabbath.

The man went away, and told the Jews that it was 15 Jesus which had made him whole. And for this cause did 16 the Jews persecute Jesus, because he did these things on the sabbath. But Jesus answered them, My Father 17 worketh even until now, and I work. For this cause 18 therefore the Jews sought the more to kill him, because he not only brake the sabbath, but also called God his own Father, making himself equal with God.

---

11. To the sick man thus healed of his infirmity, this act of Divine power rightly seemed to imply authority in the healer, even over the Sabbath. See Mark ii. 28.

14. sin no more. Jesus marks clearly that in this case at least the infirmity was a result of sin. But it would not be right to generalise from this.

17. My Father worketh even until now, and I work. The creative work of God never ceases. In spite of the Sabbath He is working unrestingly until now. In this special act Jesus was manifesting the Divine work of 'restoration of all things' to the lost perfection.

18. For this cause therefore, &c. The more Jesus manifests Himself the more intense is the hostility. It is important to note that the enemies of Jesus recognised His claim to be the Son of God.

brake, lit. was loosing, i.e. declared that the law of the Sabbath was not binding. For this sense of 'binding' and 'loosing' comp. Matt. xviii. 18.

Jesus here makes no reply to the charge of breaking the Sabbath—none at least is recorded. By the time St John wrote

19–47. A discourse of Jesus. (a) All judgment committed to
the Son. 20–29. (b) Equality with the Father testified
by five witnesses. (1) The Father Himself. (2) John
the Baptist. (3) His own works. (4) Holy Scripture.
(5) Moses.

19 Jesus therefore answered and said unto them,
Verily, verily, I say unto you, The Son can do nothing
of himself, but what he seeth the Father doing: for what
things soever he doeth, these the Son also doeth in like
20 manner. For the Father loveth the Son, and sheweth him
all things that himself doeth: and greater works than
21 these will he shew him, that ye may marvel. For as the
Father raiseth the dead and quickeneth them, even so the
22 Son also quickeneth whom he will. For neither doth the
Father judge any man, but he hath given all judgement
23 unto the Son; that all may honour the Son, even as they
honour the Father. He that honoureth not the Son
24 honoureth not the Father which sent him. Verily, verily,
I say unto you, He that heareth my word, and believeth

---

his Gospel the question of the Sabbath in the Christian Church
had long been settled. For the Christian the sacredness of the
Sabbath had been transferred to the Day of the Resurrection,
and if the Sabbath was still observed, it was observed according
to the rule of Christ.

his own Father. His Father in a special sense, one with the
Father in his Divine nature.

19. The oneness in act of the Father and the Son is here
expressed in terms of human work.

20. greater works, such as are described below—the Resurrection and the Judgment; also the manifold results of
Christian history and influence still going on, and which are still
the works of the living Christ, see ch. xiv. 12.

21. A revelation of God as one who raiseth the dead; see
Hebr. xi. 19, where A.V. wrongly inserts 'him.' Christ too is
the Author or Prince of Life, Acts iii. 15. 'If any man is in
Christ he is a new creature,' 2 Cor. v. 17.

23. In no passage is the claim to equality with the Father
more clearly stated.

24. believeth him, &c., i.e. believeth His message; to be
distinguished from 'believeth on him,' A.V.

him that sent me, hath eternal life, and cometh not into
judgement, but hath passed out of death into life. Verily, 25
verily, I say unto you, The hour cometh, and now is, when
the dead shall hear the voice of the Son of God; and they
that hear shall live. For as the Father hath life in him- 26
self, even so gave he to the Son also to have life in
himself: and he gave him authority to execute judgement, 27
because he is the Son of man. Marvel not at this: for 28
the hour cometh, in which all that are in the tombs shall
hear his voice, and shall come forth; they that have done 29
good, unto the resurrection of life; and they that have
done ill, unto the resurrection of judgement.

---

hath eternal life. Note the present tense; eternal life is
the reward of the true believer not in the future only but now.
25. the dead shall hear the voice of the Son of God, &c.
Here first the resurrection power of Christ is named. In Him
shall all be made alive, 1 Cor. xv. 22. The last Adam became
a life-giving Spirit. Also here first Jesus ascribes to Himself the
title, Son of God; a title which to an Oriental would mean,
having the nature of God, being equal with God; it would
convey no idea of inferiority or of succession, see chs. ix. 35,
x. 36, xi. 4.
26. as the Father hath life in himself, the mysterious source
of life, which lies beyond all scientific explanation, is revealed
to be in the Father and the Son. The conception, however,
of a First Cause is necessary to science also. See on ch. i. 3.
27. because he is the Son of man. As Christ saves man by
becoming man, so One who shares our nature and is 'touched
with the feeling of our infirmities' shall be our Judge. Comp.
ch. v. 22, and Heb. iv. 15, v. 2. There is a judgment for
salvation as well as a judgment for condemnation, see *v.* 29.
28. all that are in the tombs shall hear his voice. The
first clear announcement of the resurrection of individuals from
the dead; the truth was latent in the O.T. but grew more manifest
as time went on. See Pss. xvi. 10, 11, xvii. 15; Is. xxv. 8,
xxvi. 19; Hos. xiii. 14, and especially Dan. xii. 2.
29. the resurrection of judgement, for 'the resurrection of
damnation,' A.V. This passage and Acts xxiv. 15 are the only
direct assertions in N.T. of the bodily resurrection of the wicked.
It is implied Matt. x. 28; Rev. xx. 12, 13; cf. Dan. xii. 2.
(Plummer.)
It is to be noted that the miracle just wrought was a sign of
the Resurrection power of Jesus.

30 I can of myself do nothing: as I hear, I judge: and my
   judgement is righteous; because I seek not mine own
31 will, but the will of him that sent me. If I bear witness of
32 myself, my witness is not true. It is another that beareth
   witness of me; and I know that the witness which he
33 witnesseth of me is true. Ye have sent unto John, and he
34 hath borne witness unto the truth. But the witness which
   I receive is not from man: howbeit I say these things,
35 that ye may be saved. He was the lamp that burneth
   and shineth: and ye were willing to rejoice for a season
36 in his light. But the witness which I have is greater than
   that of John: for the works which the Father hath given
   me to accomplish, the very works that I do, bear witness

---

30. I can of myself do nothing, denotes absolute oneness
with the Father. Every act of Jesus is an act of God the Father.
So righteous judgment is judgment in accordance with the
Father's will.

32. It is another that beareth witness of me, i.e. God the
Father. As in *vv.* 19 and 30 the oneness of Jesus with the Father
is stated, here the distinction of the Divine Persons is recognised.
But no doubt the Jews would at once infer that Jesus was
alluding to John the Baptist: so He speaks of him as answering
their thoughts and as a concession to the weakness of their
spiritual perception.

33. he hath borne witness unto the truth. John, whom
all men regarded as a prophet, had borne witness to Christ as
One who was greater than he.

34. the witness which I receive is not from man. The witness
of the Father to the Son is decisive and paramount. To cite the
human testimony of John is a concession. Still that witness
whom you believe and trust carries the same message in regard
to me.

35. the lamp that burneth and shineth, for 'a burning and
a shining light,' A.V. A lamp that burneth is from the nature
of things temporary, and destined to extinction. The passing
witness of John is contrasted with the eternal witness of the
Father.

36. the very works that I do, bear witness of me, an
appeal to the testimony not only of signs or miracles but also to
that of the life and words of Christ. The works of Christ were
such as would flow naturally from one who was God. They
were works of creation, of mercy, of forgiveness, of power, of

of me, that the Father hath sent me. And the Father 37
which sent me, he hath borne witness of me. Ye have
neither heard his voice at any time, nor seen his form.
And ye have not his word abiding in you: for whom he 38
sent, him ye believe not. Ye search the scriptures, be- 39
cause ye think that in them ye have eternal life; and
these are they which bear witness of me; and ye will not 40

---

guidance and direction for human energy in the far-distant future
of Christendom. These are the works of Christ and they are
the works of God. Therefore they witness to His Godhead.

**37. the Father which sent me, he hath borne witness of
me.** There may be a direct reference to that voice from Heaven
pronounced at the Baptism in the Jordan: ' This is my beloved
Son in whom I am well pleased.' But the witness of the Father
does not stop here. The Father witnesses to the Son by sending
Him to do the things which He Himself does. In human affairs
he who commits a trust to another bears witness to the integrity
of that other. The king who appoints an envoy for a delicate
mission; the general who entrusts an officer with the defence
of an important outpost; the prime minister who confides a
government office to a colleague; all these bear witness to the
character of the agent selected for important work. So the
Father 'sends' the Son, entrusts Him with the mission of
salvation, and of bearing witness to Him.

his form, better than 'shape,' A.V. Comp. Philipp. ii. 6, 'who
being in the form of God counted it not a prize to be on an
equality with God,' where 'form' includes the idea of the
essential nature of God.

39. Ye search the scriptures, better than ' search the scriptures,' A.V. There could be no question as to the diligence
with which the Jews searched the scriptures. " Hillel used to
say: 'the more Law (Thorah) the more life'...He who has gotten
to himself words of the Law has gotten to himself the life of the
world to come " (cited by Bp Westcott from Taylor's *Sayings of
the Fathers*); the results of this study were unedifying. These
scholars did not search for the Christ as Philip and Nathanael
(ch. i. 45). They could not as Paul or Apollos 'shew from the
scriptures that Jesus was the Christ' (see Acts xvii. 3, xviii. 28).
But the Psalmist finds God and life through the Thorah or
Law, 'with them (thy commandments) thou hast quickened me,'
or ' given me life,' Ps. cxix. 93.

40. and, here adversative ' and yet.' Holy Scripture is also a
witness for Christ. To this witness Jesus frequently appeals:
as in the synagogue of Nazareth, Luke iv. 21; as evidence for

41 come to me, that ye may have life. I receive not glory
42 from men. But I know you, that ye have not the love of
43 God in yourselves. I am come in my Father's name, and
ye receive me not: if another shall come in his own name,
44 him ye will receive. How can ye believe, which receive
glory one of another, and the glory that *cometh* from the
45 only God ye seek not? Think not that I will accuse you
to the Father: there is one that accuseth you, *even* Moses,
46 on whom ye have set your hope. For if ye believed
47 Moses, ye would believe me; for he wrote of me. But if
ye believe not his writings, how shall ye believe my
words?

> **6** 1. Retirement to the East of the Sea of Galilee. This
> retirement of Jesus and His disciples is connected in the
> Synoptic gospels with the death of John the Baptist (Matt.
> xiv. 13, Mk vi. 30, 31), and the return of the Twelve
> from a mission. (Lk. ix. 9, 10.)

6   After these things Jesus went away to the other side
of the sea of Galilee, which is *the sea* of Tiberias.

John the Baptist, Matt. xi. 4; in the Gospel on the way to
Emmaus, Luke xxiv. 27 foll.

42. ye have not the love of God. True love of God would
have made them responsive to the voice of Christ.

43. in my Father's name, i.e. to manifest the Father.
For the name of God is that by which He is known, His
manifestation.

44. the glory...from the only God. A.V. 'from God only.'

45. To disbelieve Christ is to disbelieve Moses. Comp.
S. Luke xxiv. 27, 'Beginning from Moses and from all the
prophets, he interpreted to them in all the scriptures the things
concerning himself.' There may be a special reference to
Deut. xviii. 15, 'The Lord thy God will raise up unto thee a
prophet from the midst of thee, of thy brethren, like unto me;
unto him ye shall hearken.' The expectation of this Prophet
was as keen among the Jews as the expectation of the Christ.
Jesus teaches that the Christ and the Prophet are one and the
same, comp. also Acts iii. 22.

47. See Luke xvi. 31.

VI. 1. the sea of Tiberias, so called in this Gospel only.
Tiberias, recently built by Herod Antipas, was an important

2—14. The feeding of the 5,000. Matt. xiv. 13—21, Mk vi. 30—44, Lk. ix. 10—17. The only miracle recorded by all the Evangelists.

And a great multitude followed him, because they beheld 2 the signs which he did on them that were sick. And 3 Jesus went up into the mountain, and there he sat with his disciples. Now the passover, the feast of the Jews, was 4 at hand. Jesus therefore lifting up his eyes, and seeing 5 that a great multitude cometh unto him, saith unto Philip, Whence are we to buy bread, that these may eat? And 6 this he said to prove him : for he himself knew what he would do. Philip answered him, Two hundred penny- 7 worth of bread is not sufficient for them, that every one

---

place on the west side of the Lake, with walls 3 miles in circumference. Recent discoveries prove it to have been 'a stately city, rich, strong and splendid' (Besant, *In the City and the Land*, p. 112). As Bp Lightfoot remarks Tiberias could hardly have given its name to the Lake so early as the date of our Lord's Ministry. It is however so named by Josephus (*B. J.* III. 3. 5).

3. the mountain, the high land over the Lake of Galilee.

The scene of this miracle is beautifully described by Keble, *Christian Year*, Seventh Sunday after Trinity :

'Where over rocks and sands arise
    Proud Sirion in the Northern skies,
    And Tabor's lonely peak, 'twixt thee and noonday light,
    And far below, Gennesaret's main
Spreads many a mile of liquid plain.'

sat, or 'was sitting'; the preceding verbs are also in the imperfect tense.

4. the passover, important both as a note of time and as giving significance to the miracle which follows.

6. to prove him. Perhaps Philip's weak point lay in reliance on material resources, a want of faith and spirituality.

he himself knew, &c. For other examples of St John's insight into the mind of Christ see *v.* 64.

7. Two hundred pennyworth of bread. This was not a haphazard guess. If we take a penny or *denarius* as a day's wage (Matt. xx. 2), enough for a man and his family, St Philip's calculation will be seen to have been swift and shrewd. See the present Editor's *Horæ Biblicæ*, p. 74, where this is worked out.

8 may take a little. One of his disciples, Andrew, Simon
9 Peter's brother, saith unto him, There is a lad here, which
hath five barley loaves, and two fishes : but what are
10 these among so many ? Jesus said, Make the people sit
down. Now there was much grass in the place. So the
11 men sat down, in number about five thousand. Jesus
therefore took the loaves ; and having given thanks, he
distributed to them that were set down ; likewise also of the
12 fishes as much as they would. And when they were filled,
he saith unto his disciples, Gather up the broken pieces
13 which remain over, that nothing be lost. So they gathered
them up, and filled twelve baskets with broken pieces from
the five barley loaves, which remained over unto them
14 that had eaten. When therefore the people saw the sign
which he did, they said, This is of a truth the prophet
that cometh into the world.

15. Jesus again retires.

15   Jesus therefore perceiving that they were about to come
and take him by force, to make him king, withdrew again
into the mountain himself alone.

8. Andrew is again associated with Philip in bringing people
to Christ, ch. xii. 21, 22.

9. The lad may have offered his little store (his day's provision carried from home) in unconscious faith, certainly with
generosity, and so had his reward. His little gift was multiplied
a hundredfold.

10. much grass, a note of the season—only in the spring is
the grass green in Palestine.

13. broken pieces, an improvement on 'fragments' of the
A.V. They were pieces broken off for distribution. St John
alone records this command.

14. the prophet, whose coming was eagerly expected. This
miracle suggested 'a prophet like unto Moses' (Deut. xviii. 15).
Like Moses Jesus had given them 'bread from heaven.'

15. make him king. In these excited times the Jews were
eager to find some leader bold enough to head an insurrection
and free them from the Roman power. Josephus says, *Antiq.*
XVII. 10. 4, that 'whenever the several companies of rebels
could light upon anyone to head them he was created a king
immediately.'

16—21. Jesus walks upon the sea, Matt. xiv. 22—33; Mk vi. 45—52.

And when evening came, his disciples went down unto 16 the sea; and they entered into a boat, and were going 17 over the sea unto Capernaum. And it was now dark, and Jesus had not yet come to them. And the sea was rising 18 by reason of a great wind that blew. When therefore 19 they had rowed about five and twenty or thirty furlongs they behold Jesus walking on the sea, and drawing nigh unto the boat: and they were afraid. But he saith unto 20 them, It is I; be not afraid. They were willing therefore 21 to receive him into the boat: and straightway the boat was at the land whither they were going.

22—25. The multitudes seek Jesus.

On the morrow the multitude which stood on the other 22 side of the sea saw that there was none other boat there, save one, and that Jesus entered not with his disciples into the boat, but *that* his disciples went away alone (howbeit there came boats from Tiberias nigh unto the 23 place where they ate the bread after the Lord had given thanks): when the multitude therefore saw that Jesus was 24 not there, neither his disciples, they themselves got into the boats, and came to Capernaum, seeking Jesus. And 25

---

18. was rising, note the descriptiveness of the tense as compared with 'arose' of the A.V.

19. about five and twenty or thirty furlongs, the calculation shews the expert knowledge of the fishermen. For a similar instance see ch. xxi. 8.

21. They were willing, &c., an improvement on 'willingly received,' &c. Before this they were unwilling to receive Jesus into the boat.

22. the other side, i.e. the eastern side, near Bethsaida Julias.

23. This verse is inserted to shew how the people were able to cross over to Capernaum. Fresh boats had arrived from Tiberias, perhaps partly driven by the wind.

24. Capernaum, see Map. The site is disputed. If it be at Tell Hum, ruins of the synagogue in which Jesus spoke these memor-

when they found him on the other side of the sea, they
said unto him, Rabbi, when camest thou hither?

26—65. A Discourse, arising out of the miracle, concerning
the Bread of life.

26 Jesus answered them and said, Verily, verily, I say unto
you, Ye seek me, not because ye saw signs, but because
27 ye ate of the loaves, and were filled. Work not for the
meat which perisheth, but for the meat which abideth unto
eternal life, which the Son of man shall give unto you:
28 for him the Father, *even* God, hath sealed. They said
therefore unto him, What must we do, that we may work
29 the works of God? Jesus answered and said unto them,
This is the work of God, that ye believe on him whom he
30 hath sent. They said therefore unto him, What then
doest thou for a sign, that we may see, and believe thee?

---

able words are still to be seen; and it is significant that over the
lintel the pot of manna (see *v.* 31) and a lamb are represented.

25. when camest thou hither? These men had seen that
Jesus did not embark with His disciples and wondered how he
had crossed to Capernaum.

27. Work not for the meat which perisheth. Jesus often
founds His teaching on the scene before Him, or on a recent
incident, as from the spring (iv. 10 foll.) or the incidents of the
Feast of Tabernacles (ch. vii. 37 foll.), here from the bread of
the miracle. This explains why St John includes the sign of
feeding the 5000 in his narrative. It was the occasion which
produced this memorable discussion, the meaning of which had
disclosed itself more and more clearly as Church life went on.

meat which perisheth. Not only the actual bread of the
miracle, but all earthly aims and desires. The purport of our
Lord's words is to spiritualise life and its aims. The key to the
discourse is in *vv.* 62 and 63.

hath sealed, the seal attests and ratifies a solemn document;
so the Father has solemnly confirmed the Mission of the Son.

29. This is the work of God, &c., a great revelation. All
'the works of God' (*v.* 28) are summed up in one only—faith in
Christ Jesus, who is sent by God.

It has been noted that this verse reconciles the doctrine of
St Paul and St James as to faith and works.

30. What then doest thou for a sign? The Jews fail to
understand the higher teaching. They still ask for an external
sign. Moses they think did greater works than Jesus had done.

what workest thou? Our fathers ate the manna in the 31
wilderness; as it is written, He gave them bread out of
heaven to eat. Jesus therefore said unto them, Verily, 32
verily, I say unto you, It was not Moses that gave you the
bread out of heaven; but my Father giveth you the true
bread out of heaven. For the bread of God is that which 33
cometh down out of heaven, and giveth life unto the world.
They said therefore unto him, Lord, evermore give us this 34
bread. Jesus said unto them, I am the bread of life: he 35
that cometh to me shall not hunger, and he that believeth
on me shall never thirst. But I said unto you, that ye 36
have seen me, and yet believe not. All that which the 37
Father giveth me shall come unto me; and him that
cometh to me I will in no wise cast out. For I am come 38
down from heaven, not to do mine own will, but the will
of him that sent me. And this is the will of him that sent 39
me, that of all that which he hath given me I should lose
nothing, but should raise it up at the last day. For this 40
is the will of my Father, that every one that beholdeth

---

31. See Ps. lxxviii. 24, 25.

32. It was not Moses, &c. It was the Father and not Moses
who gave the manna, and the manna was but a symbol of the
true Bread.

the true bread out of heaven. Jesus does not appeal to the
sign or miracle so lately given, but to the inner meaning of it.

34. give us this bread. Note the close parallelism with the
request of the Samaritan woman, ch. iv. 15.

35. I am the bread of life. Another self-revelation of the
Christ—an interpretation also of history—the manna was a symbol
of the 'bread of life.'

37. Mark the steps of this great argument. The Father
giveth 'the true bread,' of which manna was a type only
(*vv.* 32, 33). Jesus reveals Himself as that true bread, in whom
the Jews believe not (*vv.* 35, 36). But all whom the Father
has given come to Him, and Christ will not cast them out.
Why? because He has come to do the Father's will. And the
Father's will is that He should lose nothing of what has been
given, but raise it up at the last day, that everyone that
beholdeth the Son and believeth should have eternal life
(*vv.* 37-40).

the Son, and believeth on him, should have eternal life;
and I will raise him up at the last day.

41   The Jews therefore murmured concerning him, because
he said, I am the bread which came down out of heaven.
42 And they said, Is not this Jesus, the son of Joseph, whose
father and mother we know? how doth he now say, I
43 am come down out of heaven? Jesus answered and said
44 unto them, Murmur not among yourselves. No man can
come to me, except the Father which sent me draw him :
45 and I will raise him up in the last day. It is written in
the prophets, And they shall all be taught of God. Every
one that hath heard from the Father, and hath learned,
46 cometh unto me. Not that any man hath seen the Father,
save he which is from God, he hath seen the Father.
47 Verily, verily, I say unto you, He that believeth hath
48 eternal life. I am the bread of life. Your fathers did eat
49

---

41. The Jews then murmured. This revelation stirs conten-
tion, and is met by the assertion that they *know* His father and
mother, therefore He cannot be the Son of God.

42. how doth he now say, &c. Observe that the contrast is
felt between an ordinary human birth and the claim to have
'come down out of heaven.'

43. Murmur not among yourselves. Such argument is vain.
The one unanswerable argument, which you do not understand,
is ' the drawing of the Father.' For those who are not drawn of
the Father, and not taught of God, the Divine birth is a hidden
mystery.

45. taught of God, see Is. liv. 13, and comp. Rom. viii. 16,
' The Spirit himself beareth witness with our spirit that we are
children of God.'

46. he which is from God. Jesus Christ alone in this sense
has seen the Father. Therefore the revelation of the Father
must come through the Son, who is the *Logos* (or Word, ch. i. 1).

48. I am the bread of life. This reiteration introduces a
deeper teaching as to the significance of 'the bread of life.'
Manna was not a bread of life : for, 'your fathers are dead.'
The bread of life therefore is the distinguishing mark of the new
life-giving Covenant. The possibility of this is explained in
language which came to be understood quite clearly in the
light of the Holy Eucharist, but which was obscure and full of

the manna in the wilderness, and they died. This is the 50
bread which cometh down out of heaven, that a man
may eat thereof, and not die. I am the living bread 51
which came down out of heaven: if any man eat of this
bread, he shall live for ever : yea and the bread which
I will give is my flesh, for the life of the world.

The Jews therefore strove one with another, saying, 52
How can this man give us his flesh to eat? Jesus 53
therefore said unto them, Verily, verily, I say unto you,
Except ye eat the flesh of the Son of man and drink his
blood, ye have not life in yourselves. He that eateth my 54
flesh and drinketh my blood hath eternal life ; and

---

offence and difficulty to those who heard it first. See below
on *v.* 53.

51. the bread which I will give is my flesh. The explanation
grows more definite. The bread of life is the flesh of Christ
sacrificed on the Cross for the life of the world. The thought
passes from the type of manna to the type of the paschal lamb.

53. Except ye eat...ye have not life in yourselves. The
words had a meaning for those who heard them at the moment of
utterance. For apart from Holy Communion there is a sense in
which the flesh of Christ could be eaten and His Blood could be
drunk. That sense, suggested by the rites of sacrifice, consists in
the spiritual absorption and assimilation of Christ by the believer.

But undoubtedly it was the Communion of the Body and
Blood of Christ in the Holy Eucharist which gave their deepest
significance to these words, and which explains St John's record
of this miracle and the discourse which followed it. Comp.
1 Cor. x. 16. It may be said to explain also the omission by
this Evangelist of any account of the Institution of the Lord's
Supper.

**54. He that eateth my flesh and drinketh my blood hath
eternal life.** The union and the identity of the sacrificer with
the sacrifice symbolised by the eating of the victim's flesh is
carried into Christian thought. So far as the closeness of the
believer's union with Christ is symbolised by the offerer's partici-
pation in the *flesh* of the victim it would be a familiar thought.
But to drink the blood of the victim would be utterly shocking
to a Jew. It was expressly forbidden (Levit. xvii. 10–12). But
the blood was the life, and spiritually to drink the blood of
Christ is to be united with Him, and to share His life. See
vv. 62, 63 below.

55 I will raise him up at the last day. For my flesh is meat
56 indeed, and my blood is drink indeed. He that eateth
my flesh and drinketh my blood abideth in me, and I in
57 him. As the living Father sent me, and I live because of
58 the Father; so he that eateth me, he also shall live because
of me. This is the bread which came down out of heaven:
not as the fathers did eat, and died: for he that eateth
59 this bread shall live for ever. These things said he in
the synagogue, as he taught in Capernaum.

60 Many therefore of his disciples, when they heard *this*,
61 said, This is a hard saying; who can hear it? But Jesus
knowing in himself that his disciples murmured at this,
62 said unto them, Doth this cause you to stumble? *What*
then if ye should behold the Son of man ascending where
63 he was before? It is the spirit that quickeneth; the
flesh profiteth nothing: the words that I have spoken

---

56. abideth in me. This is best illustrated by St Paul's
frequent phrase 'in Christ' (ἐν Χριστῷ). See Eph. i. 1, ii. 13,
and comp. 1 John iv. 12–16.

57. because of me, for 'by me,' A.V. Christ is the cause
and principle of the believer's life. See ch. xiv. 19, and comp.
'I live, and yet no longer I, but Christ liveth in me,' Gal. ii. 20.

59. in the synagogue, see *v.* 24; a synagogue, *marg.* The
article is absent in the original.

60. a hard saying. It was hard to believe that Jesus of
Nazareth was the bread that came down from heaven, or that
He could give them His flesh to eat, still more that He could
give them His blood to drink.

61. cause you to stumble, better, cause you difficulty. The
original meaning of the word is to entrap.

62. What then if ye should behold, &c. The allusion must
be to the Ascension. What the disciples find to be hard now
they will not find to be hard when Christ has ascended. They
will have witnessed the return of Christ to heaven, they will
have been taught by the Spirit, and have seen the spiritual
meaning of these words.

63. It is the spirit that quickeneth, i.e. giveth life. This
verse gives the spiritual and therefore the true interpretation of
those which precede, and so removes the difficulty of a too literal
interpretation of *v.* 53 which made Christ's words a hard saying.

unto you are spirit, and are life. But there are some of 64
you that believe not. For Jesus knew from the beginning
who they were that believed not, and who it was that
should betray him. And he said, For this cause have 65
I said unto you, that no man can come unto me, except it
be given unto him of the Father.

¶6-71. The great confession of St Peter. Comp. Matt. xvi.
13-16, Mk viii. 27-29; Lk. ix. 18-20, a different occasion
from this.

Upon this many of his disciples went back, and walked 66
no more with him. Jesus said therefore unto the twelve, 67
Would ye also go away? Simon Peter answered him, 68
Lord, to whom shall we go? thou hast the words of
eternal life. And we have believed and know that thou 69
art the Holy One of God. Jesus answered them, Did 70
not I choose you the twelve, and one of you is a devil?
Now he spake of Judas *the son* of Simon Iscariot, for he 71
it was that should betray him, *being* one of the twelve.

---

64. Some of the disciples even had not the inner light.
For Jesus knew. Another instance of St John's insight into
the mind of Christ, and of Christ's knowledge of the hearts of
men. See Acts ii. 24.
66. many of his disciples went back, the first instance of
the sifting of Christ. But the Cross was the great sifting or
stumbling-block, when all forsook Him and fled.
67. the twelve, here first so described in this Gospel.
68. to whom shall we go? the first instance of the Father's
drawing, *v.* 65.
69. thou art the Holy One of God, for 'that Christ, the Son
of the living God,' A.V. See Mk i. 24, the only other passage
where Christ is thus designated; but cp. 1 John ii. 20 and
Rev. iii. 7. In a unique sense Christ is consecrated to God.
70. one of you is a devil, a satan or *diabolus*, an adversary
of the plan of Christ. Jesus names this as a corrective of
St Peter's avowal. He could not answer for *all* of the twelve.
71. Judas the son of Simon Iscariot. Hence, according to
this, the true reading, the name Iscariot, or man of Kerioth,
belongs both to father and son. Kerioth is probably to be
identified with Kerioth-Hezron, south of Hebron. In that case
Judas Iscariot was the only non-Galilean Apostle.

7 1—9. Jesus refuses to go into Judea with his brethren.

7 And after these things Jesus walked in Galilee : for he
would not walk in Judæa, because the Jews sought to kill
2 him. Now the feast of the Jews, the feast of tabernacles,
3 was at hand. His brethren therefore said unto him,
Depart hence, and go into Judæa, that thy disciples also
4 may behold thy works which thou doest. For no man
doeth anything in secret, and himself seeketh to be
known openly. If thou doest these things, manifest
5 thyself to the world. For even his brethren did not
6 believe on him. Jesus therefore saith unto them, My
7 time is not yet come ; but your time is alway ready. The
world cannot hate you ; but me it hateth, because I

VII. 1. walked in Galilee. This retreat in Galilee lasted six
whole months, from the Feast of the Passover in April to the
Feast of Tabernacles in October.

2. the feast of tabernacles, held in commemoration of the
desert life. The rites of the feast recalled the incidents of the
wandering. On each of the eight days during which the feast
lasted water was drawn from the Siloam spring and a libation
made in the Temple to commemorate the water flowing from the
rock at Meribah. So also the candles lighted in the Temple
symbolised the pillar of fire.

3. This advice of the brethren may even have been suggested
by the enemies of Christ.

5. For even his brethren did not believe on him, for 'neither
did his brethren believe in him,' A.V. This excludes the possibility of any of the brethren being included in the number of the
Twelve. For their names see Matt. xiii. 55. Of these James,
converted after the Resurrection, was afterwards President or
Bishop of the Church in Jerusalem, and was the author of the
Epistle known by his name—perhaps the earliest of the N.T.
writings. The brethren were probably sons of Joseph by a
former marriage. Their relations with Jesus are characteristic
of elder brethren.

6. My time is not yet come. See *vv.* 8, 30, and ch. ii. 4.
It was at the feast of Passover, not at this feast, as his brethren
wished, that Jesus would 'go up' openly as the Messiah. The
brethren 'went up' among the crowd of pilgrims, as indeed Jesus
Himself did afterwards, *v.* 10.

7. cannot hate you, because the brethren had taken the
side of the world.

testify of it, that its works are evil. Go ye up unto the 8
feast: I go not up yet unto this feast; because my time
is not yet fulfilled. And having said these things unto 9
them, he abode *still* in Galilee.

7 10—12 50. Ministry in Jerusalem, 10–13. Jesus goes to the
Feast of Tabernacles in Jerusalem.

But when his brethren were gone up unto the feast, then 10
went he also up, not publicly, but as it were in secret.
The Jews therefore sought him at the feast, and said, 11
Where is he? And there was much murmuring among the 12
multitudes concerning him: some said, He is a good
man; others said, Not so, but he leadeth the multitude
astray. Howbeit no man spake openly of him for fear of 13
the Jews.

14—24. Jesus teaching in the temple argues with His adversaries.

But when it was now the midst of the feast Jesus went 14
up into the temple, and taught. The Jews therefore 15
marvelled, saying, How knoweth this man letters, having
never learned? Jesus therefore answered them, and said, 16
My teaching is not mine, but his that sent me. If any 17
man willeth to do his will, he shall know of the teaching,
whether it be of God, or *whether* I speak from myself.
He that speaketh from himself seeketh his own glory: 18
but he that seeketh the glory of him that sent him, the

---

11. The Jews therefore sought him. This excitement and
interest in the 'going up' of Jesus to the feast shew the wisdom
of our Lord's determination not to go publicly.
12. murmuring, disputation. **leadeth...astray**, see *v.* 47.
15. How knoweth this man letters? Jesus had not received
a scribe's education in the Rabbinical schools.
16. My teaching, for 'My doctrine,' A.V. Comp. Matt.
vii. 29, 'He taught them as one having authority, and not as
their scribes.'
17. he shall know of the teaching, &c., a great promise.
The knowledge of truth comes from the practice of it.

19 same is true, and no unrighteousness is in him. Did not
Moses give you the law, and *yet* none of you doeth the law?
20 Why seek ye to kill me? The multitude answered, Thou
21 hast a devil: who seeketh to kill thee? Jesus answered
and said unto them, I did one work, and ye all marvel.
22 For this cause hath Moses given you circumcision (not
that it is of Moses, but of the fathers); and on the sabbath
23 ye circumcise a man. If a man receiveth circumcision
on the sabbath, that the law of Moses may not be broken;
are ye wroth with me, because I made a man every whit
24 whole on the sabbath? Judge not according to appearance,
but judge righteous judgement.

25—36. The Pharisees seek to take Jesus.

25 Some therefore of them of Jerusalem said, Is not this
26 he whom they seek to kill? And lo, he speaketh openly,
and they say nothing unto him. Can it be that the rulers
27 indeed know that this is the Christ? Howbeit we know

---

19. the law. There is a special reference to the law of the
Sabbath. The Jews continually broke the letter of the law by
circumcising on the Sabbath.

20. a devil, Greek *daimonion*, a different word from that
rendered 'devil,' vi. 70. It is equivalent to a charge of madness
or insanity. See Mark iii. 22.

22. not that it is of Moses. Circumcision was enjoined on
Abraham as a Divine ordinance. For a similar correction of the
popular reading of history see ch. vi. 32.

23. If a man receiveth circumcision, &c. Our Lord's
argument is: 'If to circumcise on the Sabbath involves no
infringement of Sabbatical law, much less does the restoration
of a man to health do so.' The underlying principle is that the
Sabbath is made for man, and not man for the Sabbath. (Matt.
xii. 12.)

25. Is not this he, &c.? The continued immunity of Jesus
excited suspicion that after all the rulers recognised him as the
Christ. Such recognition would have immense weight. See
v. 48.

26. the rulers, the members of the Sanhedrin.

27. we know this man whence he is. According to the
Jews Jesus failed in one condition of Messiahship—they knew
His birth and origin; see ch. vi. 42, and comp. Is. liii. 5.

this man whence he is : but when the Christ cometh, no one
knoweth whence he is. Jesus therefore cried in the temple, 28
teaching and saying, Ye both know me, and know whence
I am ; and I am not come of myself, but he that sent me
is true, whom ye know not. I know him ; because I am 29
from him, and he sent me. They sought therefore to take 30
him : and no man laid his hand on him, because his hour
was not yet come. But of the multitude many believed 31
on him ; and they said, When the Christ shall come, will
he do more signs than those which this man hath done ?
The Pharisees heard the multitude murmuring these things 32
concerning him ; and the chief priests and the Pharisees
sent officers to take him. Jesus therefore said, Yet a 33
little while am I with you, and I go unto him that sent me.
Ye shall seek me, and shall not find me : and where I am, 34
ye cannot come. The Jews therefore said among them- 35
selves, Whither will this man go that we shall not find him?
will he go unto the Dispersion among the Greeks, and

---

whence, i.e. from what parentage. It was thought that the
birth of the Messiah would be so lowly that His parents would
not be known.

28. cried, in an emphatic voice and tone as making a
momentous declaration.

he that sent me is true, i.e. has a real and true existence.

29. I know him. To know the Father in this sense implies
oneness and equality with the Father.

31. Some believe on the evidence of ' signs.'

32. the chief priests would belong to the party of the
Sadducees.

33. therefore. Because of this openly hostile step Jesus saw
that the end was near. The time left to the Jews for repentance
was very short.

35. will he go unto the Dispersion ? ironical. Can this be
the Messiah who being rejected by the leaders of the nation will
go on a mission to the despised Jews of the Western Dispersion,
or even to the Gentiles? The Jews made a great distinction
between the Eastern and Western Dispersion. The first, com-
prising the settlers in Syria and Babylonia, were regarded as
equal in dignity to the Hebrews of Palestine : while the Hellenists
of the Western Dispersion, separated in language, mode of
thought and manner from the Hebrews of Palestine and dwelling

teach the Greeks? What is this word that he said, Ye
36 shall seek me, and shall not find me : and where I am,
ye cannot come?

37—44. The people dispute whether Jesus is the Christ.

37 Now on the last day, the great *day* of the feast, Jesus
stood and cried, saying, If any man thirst, let him come
38 unto me, and drink. He that believeth on me, as the
scripture hath said, out of his belly shall flow rivers of
39 living water. But this spake he of the Spirit, which they
that believed on him were to receive : for the Spirit was
40 not yet *given*; because Jesus was not yet glorified. *Some*
of the multitude therefore, when they heard these words,
41 said, This is of a truth the prophet. Others said, This is

---

in lands whose very dust defiled, were held of small account.
See 1 Peter i. 1 and James i. 1.

37. the last day, the great day of the feast. This feast
strictly speaking lasted for seven days. An eighth was added,
here called the great day of the feast. See Numb. xxix. 12, 35 ;
2 Macc. x. 6, 7 ; Joseph. *Ant.* III. 10. 4, and note on *v.* 2 of
this chapter.

If any man thirst, as the people thirsted in the wilderness.
The *direct* reference is rather to the water springing from the
rock at Meribah (Ex. xvii. 6 ; Numb. xx. 11) than to the
ceremonial of the feast.

38. as the scripture hath said. No known passage of the
O.T. precisely answers to the words cited. But the reference, as
we have seen, is to the rock in Horeb, and such passages as Ex.
xvii. 6 and Numb. xx. 11 correspond to the sense of the words.
Comp. also Is. xii. 3 ; Ezek. xlvii. 1.   **out of his belly** = from
within, from out of him. The believer has a source of life within
him. His first impulse is to preach to others. Thus St Paul
preached at Damascus after his conversion. Comp. Ps. li. 12, 13.

39. not yet glorified, not yet crucified and raised from the
dead and ascended into heaven. These 'notes' of the Evangelist
are of great interest. He records the words of Christ after
having seen their fulfilment. The life-giving stream of the Spirit
had flowed from many in St John's experience. St Stephen,
St Barnabas, and above all, St Paul, were notable examples of this.

40. these words, for 'this saying,' A.V. The reference is to
all the discourse at this time.

the prophet, the great Prophet like unto Moses who was as
eagerly expected as the Messiah, Deut. xviii. 15. As with the

the Christ. But some said, What, doth the Christ come
out of Galilee ? Hath not the scripture said that the Christ 42
cometh of the seed of David, and from Bethlehem, the
village where David was ? So there arose a division in the 43
multitude because of him. And some of them would have 44
taken him ; but no man laid hands on him.

45-52. The scribes' reply to Nicodemus.

The officers therefore came to the chief priests and 45
Pharisees ; and they said unto them, Why did ye not bring
him ? The officers answered, Never man so spake. The 46
Pharisees therefore answered them, Are ye also led astray ? 47
Hath any of the rulers believed on him, or of the Pharisees ? 48
But this multitude which knoweth not the law are accursed. 49
Nicodemus saith unto them (he that came to him before, 50

Messiah so with the Prophet, there were marks or notes by which
He could be recognised, or rejected. Jesus being supposed to
have been born in Galilee could neither be the Christ nor the
Prophet (*v.* 52).

In Acts iii. 22 St Peter identifies the Prophet with Christ, and
this was probably the prevalent view. In ch. i. 21, 25 of
this gospel the Prophet is distinguished from Elijah, who was
also expected, but only as a forerunner of Christ.

42. of the seed of David. The synoptic genealogies are an
answer to this requirement. Though genealogies of Joseph
in form there can be little doubt that they equally shew the
descent of Mary.

46. Never man so spake, an indirect evidence of the con-
vincing and authoritative character of the words and presence of
Christ.

48. Hath any of the rulers believed on him ? An attempt
to crush the truth by an appeal to authority; an argument for
the unlearned. It could not have been addressed to Nicodemus.

49. this multitude that knoweth not the law. Nothing
could exceed the contempt in which the lower people were held
by the Pharisees, they were 'the people of the earth,' or
'vermin.'

50. Nicodemus by going to Jesus (ch. iii. 1 foll.) and enquiring
of Him had acted on the principle which he here cites. The
peremptory, condensed form of the answer marks the temper in
which it was given. It is a response not to the words but to the
supposed thought of Nicodemus. The omission of the object of

51 being one of them), Doth our law judge a man, except it
52 first hear from himself and know what he doeth? They
answered and said unto him, Art thou also of Galilee?
Search, and see that out of Galilee ariseth no Prophet.

7 53—**8** 11.   The woman taken in adultery.

53
8   [And they went every man unto his own house: but
2 Jesus went unto the mount of Olives.   And early in the
morning he came again into the temple, and all the people
3 came unto him; and he sat down, and taught them.   And
the scribes and the Pharisees bring a woman taken in
4 adultery; and having set her in the midst, they say unto

'search,' and of the definite article before 'prophet,' are signs of
the passionate hastiness of the reply.   Note also that the answer
is suited to the character of Nicodemus as a scholar.   Comp.
the answer to the common people, *v.* 48.

52.   out of Galilee ariseth no Prophet, lit. 'out of Galilee
prophet ariseth not.'   This would not be true in the sense that
no prophet had come from Galilee, for Elijah, Nahum, Hosea
and Jonah were Galileans.   Nor indeed, if it were so, would it
prove that Jesus could not be the predicted Prophet.   But the
whole previous discourse had been about 'The Prophet' (see
v. 40) who is intended here also.   The absence of the definite
article may be paralleled by its absence before 'Christ' in many
places.   Both the Christ and the Prophet had come to be used
as proper names.

ariseth, i.e. *The* Prophet is not described as destined to arise
out of Galilee.   Comp. Matt. ii. 4, 'where the Christ should be
born,' lit. 'is born.'

VIII. 2–11.   The woman taken in adultery.
This passage is probably out of place here.   It interrupts the
sequence of the narrative, as viii. 12 f. follows naturally on
vii. 52.

The leading MSS. omit the passage altogether, and a large
number of the secondary authorities mark it as of doubtful
genuineness (see R.V. *marg.*).   The incident is therefore not to
be regarded as an authentic part of St John's Gospel.   Nevertheless it may be a true tradition.   In some ancient copies it
is placed after Luke xxi. 38.

3.   scribes.   Mentioned here only in this Gospel, though
frequently named in the synoptic Gospels.

him, Master, this woman hath been taken in adultery, in
the very act.   Now in the law Moses commanded us to 5
stone such: what then sayest thou of her?   And this they 6
said, tempting him, that they might have *whereof* to
accuse him.   But Jesus stooped down, and with his
finger wrote on the ground.   But when they continued 7
asking him, he lifted up himself, and said unto them, He
that is without sin among you, let him first cast a stone at
her.   And again he stooped down, and with his finger 8
wrote on the ground.   And they, when they heard it, 9
went out one by one, beginning from the eldest, *even*
unto the last: and Jesus was left alone, and the woman,
where she was, in the midst.   And Jesus lifted up himself, 10
and said unto her, Woman, where are they? did no man
condemn thee?   And she said, No man, Lord.   And 11
Jesus said, Neither do I condemn thee: go thy way;
from henceforth sin no more.]

12-20.   Christ the light of the world.   The witnesses thereto.
   A discourse with unbelievers.

   Again therefore Jesus spake unto them, saying, I am 12
the light of the world: he that followeth me shall not

---

   6.   tempting him.   If Jesus condemned the woman He would
expose Himself to the censure of the Roman government.   If
He refused to condemn, He would be accused of acting against
the authority of Moses.   It was the same dilemma in which the
Pharisees and Herodians endeavoured to place Jesus (Matt. xxii.
15 foll.).
   wrote on the ground, lit. was writing or began to write.   The
words 'as though he heard them not' (A.V.) are not in the
original, but possibly explain our Lord's motive for writing on
the ground: the repeated .action however (*v.* 8) is against this
interpretation.
   7.   He that is without sin, &c.   We must remember that these
men were not officers of the law; but Elders of the Jews, who
pretended an abhorrence of the woman's sin.   If their abhorrence
had been sincere they would have taken her before a judicial
court.
   12.   the light of the world.   Probably another reference to
the ritual of the Feast of Tabernacles, at which candles were

walk in the darkness, but shall have the light of life.
13 The Pharisees therefore said unto him, Thou bearest
14 witness of thyself; thy witness is not true. Jesus answered and said unto them, Even if I bear witness of
myself, my witness is true; for I know whence I came,
and whither I go; but ye know not whence I come, or
15 whither I go. Ye judge after the flesh; I judge no man.
16 Yea and if I judge, my judgement is true; for I am not
17 alone, but I and the Father that sent me. Yea and in
your law it is written, that the witness of two men is true.
18 I am he that beareth witness of myself, and the Father
19 that sent me beareth witness of me. They said therefore
unto him, Where is thy Father? Jesus answered, Ye know
neither me, nor my Father: if ye knew me, ye would know
20 my Father also. These words spake he in the treasury,

---

lighted to symbolise the pillar of fire in the wilderness. Thus
Jesus claims to be the Divine enlightening guide of Israel.

13. There is no attempt to impugn the claim on moral
grounds. They find no fault in Him, only bring forward an
unreal, technical objection. This objection Jesus meets (*a*) by
asserting an absolute right to bear witness—a claim addressed to
the enlightened conscience (Rom. viii. 16), (*b*) by adducing the
testimony of the Father, given through the Son.

14. Even if accentuates the argument better than 'though,'
A.V.

15. Ye judge after the flesh, by treating Jesus as an ordinary
earthly witness and ignoring the Divine character of His testimony; see ch. vii. 42.

I judge no man, i.e. I am judging no man *now*. The Jews
had been judging, rather misjudging Christ. He was simply
bearing witness to the truth. This was not a time for judgement,
but of offering salvation. Or perhaps the emphasis is on the
personal pronoun—'I by myself judge no one'; the Father
is with me, see *vv.* 16, 26.

19. They said therefore, because they were not satisfied with
the witness of the unseen Father. One of the important
therefores of this Gospel.

if ye knew me, &c. A comment on the opening words of
the Gospel. Christ as the 'Word' revealed the Father, and the
Word was God.

20. in the treasury. The treasury of the Temple was in the

as he taught in the temple: and no man took him; because
his hour was not yet come.

21-30. The judgment on those who neglect Christ.

He said therefore again unto them, I go away, and ye 21
shall seek me, and shall die in your sin: whither I go, ye
cannot come.   The Jews therefore said, Will he kill 22
himself, that he saith, Whither I go, ye cannot come?
And he said unto them, Ye are from beneath; I am from 23
above: ye are of this world; I am not of this world.   I 24
said therefore unto you, that ye shall die in your sins: for
except ye believe that I am *he*, ye shall die in your sins.
They said therefore unto him, Who art thou?   Jesus said 25
unto them, Even that which I have also spoken unto you

Court of the Women. It contained thirteen brazen coffers
(called 'trumpets') in which the gifts were placed.   It was here
that Jesus was sitting when He observed the poor widow casting
in her offering of two mites, Mark xii. 41 ; Luke xxi. 1.   Here
were lighted the great golden candelabra at the Feast of
Tabernacles.

his hour was not yet come. Comp. chs. vii. 30, xii. 1.

21. ye shall die in your sin (comp. vii. 34), the awful
sentence against the race that has sinned against conscience and
the teaching of the Spirit : 'If thou hadst known the things
that belong unto peace...but now they are hid from thine eyes'
(Luke xix. 42); comp. 1 John v. 16.   (When this Gospel was
written the Divine judgment had fallen on many thousands of
Jews at the capture of Jerusalem.)

22. Will he kill himself? Possibly this is said in severe
irony.   'Will He bring upon himself the suicide's fate, and be
cast into the lowest place in Gehenna?'   But it is doubtful
whether this was a Jewish thought about suicide (see Edersheim,
Life, &c., II. 170).   Probably the meaning is, Will He take His
own life and so pass from us?

23. It is not death that will separate between Christ and the
Jews, but the barrier of sin, the spirit of unbelief.   In order to
understand Christ His disciples must have the mind of Christ,
until then there can be no union with Him, or response to His
teaching, see 1 John v. 12.

this world, i.e. human life and society uninfluenced by God.

24. except ye believe...in your sins. See 1 John v. 13,
and comp. Acts iv. 12.

26 from the beginning. I have many things to speak and
to judge concerning you : howbeit he that sent me is true ;
and the things which I heard from him, these speak I
27 unto the world. They perceived not that he spake to
28 them of the Father. Jesus therefore said, When ye have
lifted up the Son of man, then shall ye know that I am
he, and *that* I do nothing of myself, but as the Father
29 taught me, I speak these things. And he that sent me
is with me ; he hath not left me alone ; for I do always
30 the things that are pleasing to him. As he spake these
things, many believed on him.

---

25. from the beginning, i.e. from the beginning of the
ministry. The whole Gospel had been a revelation of Christ.
Dr Field has an interesting rendering here, following St Augustine,
'that I should even speak to you at all!' i.e. you are unworthy
even to have me speak to you at all, much more to be told who
I am.

26. Closely connected with *v.* 24. He has many things to
say in regard to that judgment.

27. perceived not. For Jesus had not expressly named the
Father, *v.* 26. Another note by the Evangelist.

28. When ye have lifted up, &c., see ch. iii. 14, where, as
here, lifted up combines the thought of raising on the Cross, and
of glorifying. This recognition of Jesus as the Christ took place
in large measure on the Day of Pentecost, comp. Acts ii. 35.
After St Peter's speech the conviction came home to the Jews,
who 'were pricked in their hearts.'

30, 31. many believed on him...believed him. Note this distinction. To believe *on* Jesus is to trust Him wholly, to respond
fully to His teaching. 'To believe Jesus' is to accept Him as a
teacher without full understanding of Him. These men, as the
following verses shew, had not laid aside their prejudices or false
views of the Messiah and the Kingdom of God. As the words
which follow, down to *v.* 58, were addressed to 'those who had
believed Him,' it is clear that many professed discipleship
without understanding the spirit of Christ's teaching and without
casting off their Jewish prejudices : they tried to bring Judaism
into Christianity. The temper and attitude of these men enable
us to understand the excesses of the Judaizing party in the early
Church, and also the speedy and awful corruption of the Church
described, e.g. 2 Peter ii. and Jude. Comp. Acts xv. 5, when
certain of the sect of the Pharisees 'that believed' tried to force

31–59. Jesus argues with those who 'believed him,' but were yet unenlightened.

Jesus therefore said to those Jews which had believed 31 him, If ye abide in my word, *then* are ye truly my disciples; and ye shall know the truth, and the truth 32 shall make you free. They answered unto him, We be 33 Abraham's seed, and have never yet been in bondage to any man: how sayest thou, Ye shall be made free? Jesus 34 answered them, Verily, verily, I say unto you, Every one that committeth sin is the bondservant of sin. And the 35 bondservant abideth not in the house for ever: the son abideth for ever. If therefore the Son shall make you 36 free, ye shall be free indeed. I know that ye are 37 Abraham's seed; yet ye seek to kill me, because my word hath not free course in you. I speak the things 38

---

circumcision on the Church; just as these Jews attempted to bring Jewish prejudices into their belief.

31 foll. Probably a fresh discourse.

32. the truth shall make you free. Truth in this sense is conformity to the will of God. If Israel had accepted Jesus as the Christ the truth would have given them the freedom which Christ possessed. No man in the whole Roman Empire was so free as Christ. Neither Jew nor Roman made Him swerve for an instant or a hair's-breadth from His purpose; which was to do His Father's will; 'whose service is perfect freedom' (cui servire regnare est).

33. never yet been in bondage to any man. The past history of Israel seems to belie this. But it was not so much political subjection as actual slavery, and not so much the past as the present that they were thinking of. In that sense they were free. But, as always, the meaning of Christ was spiritual: the Jews were in bondage to sin, comp. Rom. vi. 18, 22, and viii. 2. This was Israel's great opportunity. If they had accepted truth in Christ as a nation the Jews would have possessed the moral sovereignty of the world.

34. Jesus answered them, first by shewing in what sense they had been slaves, *vv.* 34–36. Secondly by shewing how they failed to be true children of Abraham, *vv.* 37–40.

37. hath not free course in you, better, as in *marg.*, 'hath no place in you,' as it had in Abraham, who therefore would not have sought to slay the Christ. Comp. Matt. xix. 11, where the same verb is used in a transitive sense.

which I have seen with *my* Father: and ye also do the
39 things which ye heard from *your* father. They answered
and said unto him, Our father is Abraham. Jesus saith
unto them, If ye were Abraham's children, ye would do
40 the works of Abraham. But now ye seek to kill me, a
man that hath told you the truth, which I heard from
41 God: this did not Abraham. Ye do the works of your
father. They said unto him, We were not born of
42 fornication; we have one Father, *even* God. Jesus said
unto them, If God were your Father, ye would love me:
for I came forth and am come from God; for neither have
43 I come of myself, but he sent me. Why do ye not understand my speech? *Even* because ye cannot hear my
44 word. Ye are of *your* father the devil, and the lusts of
your father it is your will to do. He was a murderer
from the beginning, and stood not in the truth, because
there is no truth in him. When he speaketh a lie, he
speaketh of his own: for he is a liar, and the father

---

40. this did not Abraham, for he recognised the true
character of God, and therefore would know that Jesus was God.
This is also the argument of *v.* 42.

42, 43. These two verses contain two great principles which
underlie our Lord's attitude towards the Jews. (*a*) One principle
(*v.* 42) is that in the O.T. Scriptures the Jews were in possession of
a key to the recognition of Christ as the Son of God which made
them responsible for their rejection of Him. If they truly understood the character of God in the O.T. they would recognise in
Jesus the impress and image of the Godhead. For illustration of
this comp. Acts xiii. 27, 'They that dwell in Jerusalem, and their
rulers, because they knew him not, nor the voices of the prophets,'
&c.

(*b*) The second principle, *v.* 43, is that in every truly religious
soul there is latent a faculty by which the Godhead may be
recognised. See 1 John iii. 24; Rom. viii. 16; 1 Cor. ii.
13–16, iii. 16. Without that principle a man cannot know God
or hear His voice.

44. the devil, the satan or adversary of God—the true
meaning of the Greek word; see Numb. xxii. 22, διαβαλεῖν αὐτόν.

a murderer. As God is the source of life, so through the
devil came death. **A liar and the father thereof.** The devil is

thereof. But because I say the truth, ye believe me not. 45
Which of you convicteth me of sin? If I say truth, why 46
do ye not believe me? He that is of God heareth the 47
words of God: for this cause ye hear *them* not, because
ye are not of God. The Jews answered and said unto 48
him, Say we not well that thou art a Samaritan, and hast
a devil? Jesus answered, I have not a devil; but I honour 49
my Father, and ye dishonour me. But I seek not mine 50
own glory: there is one that seeketh and judgeth. Verily, 51
verily, I say unto you, If a man keep my word, he shall
never see death. The Jews said unto him, Now we know 52
that thou hast a devil. Abraham is dead, and the
prophets; and thou sayest, If a man keep my word, he
shall never taste of death. Art thou greater than our 53
father Abraham, which is dead? and the prophets are
dead: whom makest thou thyself? Jesus answered, If 54

---

the author and suggester of false aims and views of life: and false
views of God and Christ. Note how clearly Christ teaches
here the personality of Satan.

45. because I say the truth. That which *ought* to create
conviction produces disbelief.

46. convicteth me of sin? A great improvement on A.V.
'convinceth.' It is a word that no other than He could have
spoken in sincerity. This is an appeal by Jesus to His own
sinlessness; comp. 1 Peter ii. 22, 'who did no sin, neither was
guile found in his mouth.' The only attempted answer is given
in *v.* 48, and that answer is groundless slander.

47. See above on *vv.* 42 and 43 (*b*).

48. art a Samaritan, and hast a devil, or demon, *marg.*
Edersheim points out that the word 'Samaritan' (*Shomron*) was
a name given to the prince of the demons. (*Life*, &c., II. 174.)
The two expressions are therefore equivalent. The answer is a
mere *tu quoque.*

49. Jesus replies by a calm denial; see 1 Peter ii. 23, 'who
when he was reviled, reviled not again...but committed himself
to him that judgeth righteously.'

51. See *v.* 31. Here the same promise is repeated in other
words.

53. Art thou greater than our father Abraham? As the
giver of life (*v.* 51) Jesus claimed for Himself the possession of

I glorify myself, my glory is nothing: it is my Father that
55 glorifieth me; of whom ye say, that he is your God; and
ye have not known him: but I know him; and if I should
say, I know him not, I shall be like unto you, a liar: but
56 I know him, and keep his word. Your father Abraham
57 rejoiced to see my day; and he saw it, and was glad. The
Jews therefore said unto him, Thou art not yet fifty years
58 old, and hast thou seen Abraham? Jesus said unto them,
Verily, verily, I say unto you, Before Abraham was, I am.
59 They took up stones therefore to cast at him: but Jesus
hid himself, and went out of the temple.

---

eternal life—a prerogative greater than Abraham could boast
of.

56. Your father Abraham rejoiced to see my day, &c. One
of the promises to Abraham was that in his seed all the families
of the earth should be blessed (Gen. xxii. 18). He rejoiced in
the prospect of seeing that day (see *marg.* ' that he should see ').
Though the literal fulfilment did not come during Abraham's life
on earth, it is possible that his faith shewn in the sacrifice of
Isaac may have been rewarded by some clear revelation of the
purpose of God not recorded in Genesis. Many commentators
see in these words a revelation by Jesus Christ of the unseen
world and the presence of Abraham there. Of this Bishop
Westcott says, ' the tense of the original is decisive against this
view.'

57. and hast thou seen Abraham? Jesus does not exactly
answer this question, but makes the momentous revelation of
His eternal pre-existence in the words, ' Before Abraham was,
I am.'

58. Before Abraham was, I am. The twofold assertion of
eternal pre-existence, and of Divine nature, is unmistakable. The
action of the Jews (*v.* 59) proves clearly what the import of the
words was to them. ' I am ' was understood to be the Divine
name of Exodus iii. 14.

59. went out of the temple. A.V. adds 'going through
the midst of them and so passed by.' But the best MS. authority
is against the insertion of these words.

This is the conclusion of the last great appeal of Jesus to the
Jews before His passion. Some responded to the appeal (*v.* 30),
but most rejected it.

9 1-41. The healing of a man blind from his birth, and the
consequences of it.

And as he passed by, he saw a man blind from his birth. **9**
And his disciples asked him, saying, Rabbi, who did sin, 2
this man, or his parents, that he should be born blind?
Jesus answered, Neither did this man sin, nor his parents: 3
but that the works of God should be made manifest in
him. We must work the works of him that sent me, 4
while it is day: the night cometh, when no man can work.

IX. 1. This is one of the seven great miracles or signs of Christ
recorded by St John. Each is a manifestation of the Word or
logos, and six of them are signs of the creative power of God.
This miracle in particular is important: (1) as marking a crisis
in the hostility of the Jews: (2) as the first instance of persecution,
or witnessing to Christ, i.e. of martyrdom: (3) as directly
leading to the foundation of the Church.

a man blind from his birth. Comp. Acts iii. 2. This
circumstance made the cure in both cases more wonderful. His
parents are questioned on this point, *v.* 19. From *v.* 8 we learn
that the blind man was a beggar, sitting probably at one of the
gates of the Temple. This day, being the Sabbath, he does not
ask alms, or, like Bartimaeus, pray to Jesus, of whom indeed he
was ignorant. Even after the cure He is to him at first only
'the man called Jesus,' *v.* 11.

2. Rabbi. Teacher, lit. my great one.

who did sin, &c. ? An instance of the kind of question
discussed in Rabbinical schools. See Lightfoot, *Horæ Hebraicæ
ad loc.*

3. Jesus answered, &c. Jesus by one word rejects both
alternatives in this case. He states a cause which is full of
mystery and suggestiveness.

This man was born to suffering in order that the glory of God
might be manifested. How often may this be the explanation of
Christian lives, in which suffering borne with patience witnesses
for Christ.

4. We must work, for 'I must work,' A.V. Not only the
disciples of Christ but all His servants in every age are included
in the thought.

the night cometh, when no man can work. Not only are the
special works of Christ's ministry limited to His time on earth,
but each Christian has his special work to do *here* and *now.*

5 When I am in the world, I am the light of the world.
6 When he had thus spoken, he spat on the ground, and made clay of the spittle, and anointed his eyes with the
7 clay, and said unto him, Go, wash in the pool of Siloam (which is by interpretation, Sent). He went away there-
8 fore, and washed, and came seeing. The neighbours therefore, and they which saw him aforetime, that he was a beggar, said, Is not this he that sat and begged?
9 Others said, It is he : others said, No, but he is like him.
10 He said, I am *he*. They said therefore unto him, How
11 then were thine eyes opened? He answered, The man that is called Jesus made clay, and anointed mine eyes, and said unto me, Go to Siloam, and wash : so I went

---

5. When I am in the world, includes both past ages and the present. It is often noted how any fresh movement for good in thought or action takes its light and inspiration from Christ. See *Jesus Christ and the Social Question*, Peabody, p. 71 foll.

the light of the world, see ch. i. 4, 5, 9, and viii. 12. The title is here named with singular beauty and appropriateness.

6. he spat on the ground. 'The use of saliva was a well-known Jewish remedy for diseases of the eyes,' Edersheim, *Life,* &c., II. 48.

made clay. To do this on the Sabbath-day was an unlawful act according to Pharisaic rules.

7. Go, wash in the pool of Siloam. This command would be a test of faith, a necessary condition for working a miracle of healing. The Pool of Siloam (in O.T. Shiloah, Is. viii. 6), now called the *Birket Silwân*, was situated to the S. of Jerusalem at the junction of the Tyropoeon Valley and the Valley of Hinnom. In the time of our Lord it was surrounded by a covered arcade; it was a fountain as well as a pool. The derivation from *Shalach,* 'to send,' points to the former rather than to the latter. Its original dimensions were 71 ft from N. to S. by 75 ft from E. to W. For the symbolic meaning of this stream or fount see Isaiah viii. 6, and Ps. xlvi. 4.

9. This vivid description of hesitating recognition points to an eye-witness, probably the Evangelist himself. Comp. Acts iii. 10, 'took knowledge,' i.e. gradually recognised the lame man.

11. He answered, &c. This clear, direct statement of fact, without inference at first, is characteristic. The story is told even more briefly and pointedly *v.* 15.

The man, for 'a man' A.V.

away and washed, and I received sight. And they said 12
unto him, Where is he? He saith, I know not.

They bring to the Pharisees him that aforetime was 13
blind. Now it was the sabbath on the day when Jesus 14
made the clay, and opened his eyes. Again therefore the 15
Pharisees also asked him how he received his sight. And
he said unto them, He put clay upon mine eyes, and I
washed, and do see. Some therefore of the Pharisees 16
said, This man is not from God, because he keepeth not
the sabbath. But others said, How can a man that is
a sinner do such signs? And there was a division
among them. They say therefore unto the blind man 17
again, What sayest thou of him, in that he opened thine
eyes? And he said, He is a prophet. The Jews therefore 18
did not believe concerning him, that he had been blind,
and had received his sight, until they called the parents
of him that had received his sight, and asked them, 19
saying, Is this your son, who ye say was born blind?
how then doth he now see? His parents answered and 20
said, We know that this is our son, and that he was born
blind: but how he now seeth, we know not; or who opened 21
his eyes, we know not: ask him; he is of age; he shall

---

13. They bring to the Pharisees, &c. in order that a charge
against Jesus of breaking the Sabbath might be founded on this
man's evidence. The two charges are named in the next verse.

14. Now it was the sabbath. See ch. v. 9.

16. How can a man that is a sinner do such signs? This
argument perhaps marks the influence of Nicodemus among the
Pharisees: there were some who thought with him. See iii. 2,
and *v.* 33 below.

18. The first attempt was to deny or disparage the wonder of
the cure, to make it out to be a deception, or an ordinary case of
healing.

20. His parents answered and said, &c. The simplicity and
directness of the evidence both of the son and of his parents are
striking. Mark too the caution at first (the name of Christ is
never mentioned), and then the growing boldness, first in statement, *v.* 25, then in inference, *v.* 31, and argument, *v.* 33.

21. he is of age. Up to twelve years of age a Jewish boy
would be held wholly irresponsible for his actions.

22 speak for himself. These things said his parents, because
they feared the Jews : for the Jews had agreed already,
that if any man should confess him *to be* Christ, he should
23 be put out of the synagogue. Therefore said his parents,
24 He is of age ; ask him. So they called a second time the
man that was blind, and said unto him, Give glory to
25 God : we know that this man is a sinner. He therefore
answered, Whether he be a sinner, I know not : one thing
26 I know, that, whereas I was blind, now I see. They said
therefore unto him, What did he to thee ? how opened he
27 thine eyes ? He answered them, I told you even now,
and ye did not hear : wherefore would ye hear it again ?
28 would ye also become his disciples ? And they reviled
him, and said, Thou art his disciple ; but we are disciples
29 of Moses. We know that God hath spoken unto Moses :
30 but as for this man, we know not whence he is. The man
answered and said unto them, Why, herein is the marvel,

----

22. he should be put out of the synagogue. A terrible
sentence. An excommunicated man was 'like one dead. He
was not allowed to study with others, no intercourse was to be
held with him, he was not even to be shewn the road. He
might indeed buy the necessaries of life, but it was forbidden
to eat or drink with such an one.' Edersheim, *Life*, &c., II.
184.

24. Give glory to God. A formula for exacting confession,
comp. Josh. vii. 19.

we know that this man is a sinner. The attempt to force
denial by authority is characteristic of all persecuting tribunals.

Nowhere else perhaps is the issue brought so directly to the
point between the truth of Christ and the tradition of the
Pharisees.

26. What did he to thee ? how opened he thine eyes ? The
enquiry is pressed and repeated, in order probably to elicit some
compromising incident in the miracle. But the man is firm in his
facts, and the argument only deepens his conviction that Jesus
is of God, *v.* 33.

27. ye did not hear. They failed to understand the meaning
of this act.

29. we know not whence he is. See ch. viii. 14.

30. Why, herein is the marvel, &c. Note the growing boldness of the man. He begins now to argue from his facts. An
advance on *vv.* 11 and 15.

that ye know not whence he is, and *yet* he opened mine
eyes. We know that God heareth not sinners: but if 31
any man be a worshipper of God, and do his will, him he
heareth. Since the world began it was never heard that 32
any one opened the eyes of a man born blind. If this 33
man were not from God, he could do nothing. They 34
answered and said unto him, Thou wast altogether
born in sins, and dost thou teach us? And they cast
him out.

Jesus heard that they had cast him out; and finding 35
him, he said, Dost thou believe on the Son of God? He 36
answered and said, And who is he, Lord, that I may
believe on him? Jesus said unto him, Thou hast both 37
seen him, and he it is that speaketh with thee. And 38

---

31. We know that God heareth not sinners. This is a
principle which the Pharisees not only admitted, but strongly
affirmed and taught. The argument was unanswerable.

32. Since the world began, &c. A sense of something greater
in the Healer than mere freedom from sin dawns on the man's
consciousness. The act was unparalleled.

33, 34. One of the despised 'people of the earth' teaches
simply by clinging to the fact and the clear inference from it—
a proof that the 'sign' was a manifestation of the Word or
Logos.

34. born in sins, see *v.* 2. The Pharisees answer the question
in their own way.

cast him out. See above, *v.* 22. Thus this man becomes
the first sufferer for Christ's sake; the first to gain the promise
of the 'Beatitudes,' Matt. v. 10, 12.

35. finding him, in his moment of despair, an outcast for
conscience' sake from all human society. Jesus reveals Himself
to this bold and truthful confessor, as He did to the woman of
Samaria.

Dost thou believe, &c., the foundation truth of the Church
is that Jesus is the Son of God (Matt. xvi. 16). By ac-
knowledgment of this truth this man cured of his blindness
becomes a member of the Church of Christ and its first Martyr
or Confessor.

A few very important MSS. and some versions read 'Son of
Man,' which Bp Westcott prefers to the reading of R.V. See
his additional note on this chapter.

he said, Lord, I believe. And he worshipped him.
39 And Jesus said, For judgement came I into this world, that
they which see not may see ; and that they which see
40 may become blind. Those of the Pharisees which were
with him heard these things, and said unto him, Are we
41 also blind? Jesus said unto them, If ye were blind, ye
would have no sin : but now ye say, We see : your sin
remaineth.

10 1–18. Jesus reveals Himself (a) as the Shepherd of His
Sheep ; (b) as the Door of the Sheepfold ; (c) as the Good
Shepherd, who layeth down his life for the sheep.

10 Verily, verily, I say unto you, He that entereth not by

---

38. Lord, I believe. The conviction had already come home
to the man. It only needed expression. As an illustration of
growing faith, and of progress from the knowledge of 'the man
named Jesus,' to belief in the Son of God, the narrative is most
suggestive.

worshipped him as God.

39. which see not. 'The multitude that knoweth not the
law,' ch. vii. 49 ; the 'babes' in Christ, Luke x. 22.

they which see, i.e. the Pharisees, who think themselves
enlightened. Comp. Isaiah xlii. 19, 'Who is blind, but my
servant? or deaf, as my messenger that I send?'

40. Those of the Pharisees which were with him for 'some
of the Pharisees, &c.' A.V. These were the 'Jews who believed
Him' (not on Him), ch. viii. 30, 31, whose faith was imperfect.

41. now ye say, We see, &c. The Pharisees were guilty
because they sinned against light. They held to their traditions
in spite of the evidence of the truth of Christ. They claimed
to 'see,' but in reality they were blind.

Ch. X. Three parables or allegories concerning the future of
the Church. (1) There is one true Shepherd or Chief Pastor
of the Church, 1–6. (2) Jesus reveals Himself as the 'door of
the sheep.' Others who had entered the fold were thieves
and robbers, 7–10. (3) The care and devotion of the Good
Shepherd for His flock, in contrast to the hirelings, 11–16. In
this He and the Father are in perfect sympathy, 17, 18.

There is a close connexion between these parables and the
preceding incident which is alluded to in *v.* 21 of this chapter.
Our Lord reveals Himself as the Chief Pastor of His Church.
We see the germs of a Christian Church in the cured man

the door into the fold of the sheep, but climbeth up some
other way, the same is a thief and a robber. But he that 2
entereth in by the door is the shepherd of the sheep. To 3
him the porter openeth ; and the sheep hear his voice :
and he calleth his own sheep by name, and leadeth them
out. When he hath put forth all his own, he goeth before 4
them, and the sheep follow him : for they know his voice.
And a stranger will they not follow, but will flee from 5
him : for they know not the voice of strangers. This 6
parable spake Jesus unto them : but they understood not
what things they were which he spake unto them.

Jesus therefore said unto them again, Verily, verily, 7
I say unto you, I am the door of the sheep. All that 8

---

separated from the Jewish community through his faith in
Christ ; and 'found' by Him (ix. 35). The contrast therefore
between the 'good shepherd' and the 'hireling' is a contrast
between Christ and the misguided teachers of Israel.

X. 1. the fold of the sheep. An Eastern sheepfold is
surrounded by a high wall. The entrance is by a door closed
at night and guarded by a porter. Several flocks may be
driven into one fold for safety at night. In the morning each
shepherd calls his sheep and they follow him.

a thief and a robber. The reference must be to the Pharisees
and other false teachers who misguided the Jewish people.

3. the porter openeth, in the interpretation the porter may
represent S. John the Baptist, who recognised the Christ and
opened the way to Him. But the meaning may well be extended
to all who through the Holy Spirit prepare the way for Christ,
and open the door of His Church.

calleth his own sheep by name. In a fold there may be
sheep belonging to different shepherds. It was not all the Jews
who recognised Jesus or heard His voice. Comp. Is. xliii. 1, ' I
have called thee by thy name, thou art mine.'

leadeth them out. In other words Jesus Christ constitutes
His Church ; He calls His own forth from the Jewish theocracy.
Comp. Acts ii. 39, ' As many as the Lord our God shall call.'

7. therefore, because they did not understand the meaning
of the first parable Jesus speaks more plainly.

the door of the sheep, i.e. the door by which the sheep enter
the fold. The one entrance into the Church is through Christ,
not through Judaism. Hence baptism in the name of Jesus
Christ is the first and necessary step for admission, Acts ii. 38.

came before me are thieves and robbers : but the sheep
9 did not hear them.   I am the door : by me if any man
enter in, he shall be saved, and shall go in and go out,
10 and shall find pasture.   The thief cometh not, but that he
may steal, and kill, and destroy : I came that they may
11 have life, and may have *it* abundantly.   I am the good
shepherd : the good shepherd layeth down his life for the
12 sheep.   He that is a hireling, and not a shepherd, whose

---

8. thieves and robbers. See *v.* 1.
did not hear them. The true Israelite made no response to
the false teaching of the Pharisees, who are represented as
'stealing, killing and destroying' (*v.* 10), i.e. making void the
word of God through their traditions, Matt. xv. 6. Comp.
Mark vii. 9. Comp. also 'the letter (of Pharisaism) kills, the
spirit (of Christ) giveth life,' 2 Cor. iii. 6.
Godet notes that 'the first picture is bright with the hues of
morning, the second depicts the active midday life, the third is an
evening scene, when the flocks find safety in the fold from the
attacks of wolves.'
9. shall be saved. So the first disciples are spoken of as
'those that were being saved' (or, 'seeking to save themselves,'
comp. Thuc. VII. 44), Acts ii. 47.   **go in and go out.** The
Christian is free to go forth into the world, and **find pasture,**
i.e. turn to account all that is best on earth ; comp. Phil. iv. 8,
and see Westcott *ad loc.*
10. The thief is the unworthy servant of Christ, who for
selfish ends ruins the life of Christ's flock. Christ is the giver of
life in all its fulness.
11. the good shepherd. The word for 'good' is the same
as that used for a 'good' work, Matt. xxvi. 10. It implies fitness for the end in view, beauty and attractiveness.
Here fitness consists in the shepherd's readiness to lay down
(or 'give' A.V.) his life for his sheep. See Is. xl. 11 ; Ezek.
xxxiv. 23.
layeth down his life for the sheep. It was the hatred of
the Pharisees—the wolves of the last parable—that more than
anything else brought about the death of Jesus. In opposing
them He laid down His life for the sheep.
12. He that is a hireling. The reference is perhaps princi-
pally to the chief priests and Sadducees, who were the official
(hired) guardians of religion, but who had not the courage to
oppose the corrupting influence of Pharisaism. Comp. ch. xii.
42, 'Even of the rulers many believed on him ; but because of

own the sheep are not, beholdeth the wolf coming, and
leaveth the sheep, and fleeth, and the wolf snatcheth
them, and scattereth *them* : *he fleeth* because he is a 13
hireling, and careth not for the sheep. I am the good 14
shepherd ; and I know mine own, and mine own know
me, even as the Father knoweth me, and I know the 15
Father ; and I lay down my life for the sheep. And 16
other sheep I have, which are not of this fold : them also
I must bring, and they shall hear my voice ; and they
shall become one flock, one shepherd. Therefore doth 17
the Father love me, because I lay down my life, that
I may take it again. No one taketh it away from me, 18
but I lay it down of myself. I have power to lay it down,
and I have power to take it again. This commandment
received I from my Father.

the Pharisees they did not confess it, lest they should be put out
of the synagogue.'

14. In this verse Jesus passes from parable to the facts of His
ministry.

the good shepherd as opposed to the hirelings as well as to the
wolves. He cares for the sheep as well as defends them.

I know mine own, for, 'I know my sheep,' A.V.

16. other sheep...not of this fold. The allusion undoubtedly
is to those among the pagans or Gentiles whose souls were
'naturally Christian'; whom Christ would also bring into His
Church. Comp. Acts xxviii. 28, 'This salvation of God is sent
unto the Gentiles : they will also hear.'

This admission of the Gentiles into the Christian Church is
what S. Paul calls 'a mystery,' the Divine plan hidden for ages,
revealed in the latter days.

one flock, one shepherd. Note this important correction of
A.V. which reads 'one fold.' There are many 'folds' in the
Church of Christ, many national Churches; but there is one
flock, one Catholic Church, under One Shepherd : comp. Hebr.
xiii. 20. 'The translation of "fold" for "flock" has been most
disastrous in idea, and in influence,' Westcott *ad loc.*

17. I lay down my life. Jesus repeats the word already
uttered, *v.* 11, in order to shew the wholly voluntary character of
His sacrifice for man, and the approval of it by the Father.

that I may take it again. The love of the Father requires
the continuance of the eternal life of the Son.

18. This commandment, this charge or privilege of complete
freedom in laying down His life and of taking it again.

19–21. A further dispute as to whether Jesus is the Christ.

19   There arose a division again among the Jews because
20 of these words. And many of them said, He hath a devil,
21 and is mad ; why hear ye him ? Others said, These are
not the sayings of one possessed with a devil. Can a devil
open the eyes of the blind ?

22–39. The Feast of the Dedication. Jesus reveals Himself as
One with the Father.

22   And it was the feast of the dedication at Jerusalem :
23 it was winter ; and Jesus was walking in the temple in
24 Solomon's porch. The Jews therefore came round about

19, 20. There arose a division, &c. A vague charge of
madness is all that can be raised against the impression created
by the wonderful words of Jesus, and the evidence of the
miracle.

22. the feast of the dedication, mentioned by St John only
in N.T. It was held towards the end of December, two months
later than the Feast of Tabernacles, and was instituted by Judas
Maccabaeus to commemorate the dedication of the new altar of
burnt sacrifice after the profanation of the Temple and of the old
altar by Antiochus Epiphanes in 165 B.C. It lasted eight days
and was a time of great rejoicing. It was sometimes called
'the feast of lights.' See ch. viii. 12. As a feast of national
deliverance it gives point to the question in *v.* 24.

After the Feast of Tabernacles Jesus probably withdrew to
Galilee, and thence made this short visit to Jerusalem for the
Feast of the Dedication. The visit to Martha and Mary, Luke x.
38–42, and the parable of the Good Samaritan, may be assigned
to this period ; after which Jesus again returned to Galilee, where
He remained until His last journey to Jerusalem. This period
between the Feast of Tabernacles and the Passover occupies
St Luke ix. 51—xviii. 18.

23. was walking, better than 'walked,' A.V.

in Solomon's porch. The Temple area was surrounded by lofty
colonnades or porticoes. Solomon's Porch was on the eastern
side overlooking the Valley of Jehoshaphat. It was also a place
of resort for the disciples of Christ after the Resurrection,
Acts iii. 11. Note as a point of local knowledge that St John
speaks of Solomon's Porch as being well known to him, whereas
St Luke describes it as 'the porch that is called Solomon's.'
These notes of special localities go far to disprove the supposition that this Gospel was written in the second century by a

him, and said unto him, How long dost thou hold us in
suspense? If thou art the Christ, tell us plainly. Jesus 25
answered them, I told you, and ye believe not : the works
that I do in my Father's name, these bear witness of me.
But ye believe not, because ye are not of my sheep. My 26
sheep hear my voice, and I know them, and they follow 27
me : and I give unto them eternal life ; and they shall 28
never perish, and no one shall snatch them out of my
hand. My Father, which hath given *them* unto me, is 29
greater than all ; and no one is able to snatch *them* out of

---

disciple of St John unfamiliar with Palestine. All such local
features had been obliterated by the destruction of Jerusalem
under Titus in A.D. 70, and would be difficult to recover. The
mention of the Treasury is another instance of this local
knowledge.

24. hold us in suspense, for 'make us to doubt,' A.V. By
a similar expression Thucydides describes the condition of
trembling uncertainty in which all Greece found itself before the
outbreak of the Peloponnesian War, Thuc. II. 8.

tell us plainly. Jesus never said plainly to the Jews, 'I am
the Christ.' He manifests Himself to those who understand the
Christ as revealed in the Old Testament, who could say with
Philip (ch. i. 45), 'We have found him of whom Moses in the
law, and the prophets, did write.' To say 'I am the Christ' to
unbelieving Jews would be misleading. For the Christ as they
conceived Him was not the true Christ.

There were two whom He 'told plainly,'—the Samaritan
woman and the blind man (chs. iv. 26 and ix. 37).

26. because ye are not of my sheep, a reference to the three
parables spoken two months previously. The conception of a
Church separate from the Jewish community has become definite.
They only could respond to Jesus who had 'the mind of Christ'
(1 Cor. ii. 16).

27, 28. Note how precisely these verses recall the incidents
of each of the three parables *vv.* 1–16. *v.* 27 recalls the first
parable, *v.* 28 *a* the second, *v.* 28 *b* the third.

29. no one is able...Father's hand. This beautiful expression
of the Father's love is characteristic of the Gospel, especially of
this Gospel. It is a revelation of the Fatherhood of God which
far exceeds that of the Old Covenant. It is a Fatherhood, which
even sin cannot alienate. 'When the sinner turns to his Father
he finds that the Father has been waiting for him' (Dr Swete).

³⁰
³¹ the Father's hand. I and the Father are one. The Jews
³² took up stones again to stone him. Jesus answered them,
Many good works have I shewed you from the Father;
³³ for which of those works do ye stone me? The Jews
answered him, For a good work we stone thee not, but
for blasphemy; and because that thou, being a man,
³⁴ makest thyself God. Jesus answered them, Is it not
³⁵ written in your law, I said, Ye are gods? If he called them
gods, unto whom the word of God came (and the scripture
³⁶ cannot be broken), say ye of him, whom the Father
sanctified and sent into the world, Thou blasphemest;
³⁷ because I said, I am *the* Son of God? If I do not the
³⁸ works of my Father, believe me not. But if I do them,
though ye believe not me, believe the works: that ye may
know and understand that the Father is in me, and I in
³⁹ the Father. They sought again to take him: and he
went forth out of their hand.

---

30. I and the Father are one. Although the great truth
may be certainly inferred from ch. i. 'the Word was God,' *v.* 1,
and 'the Word became flesh,' *v.* 14, it is here more decisively
stated. One, not only in power and will, but one in nature and
essence.

33. thou, being a man, makest thyself God. No disciple of
Jesus could have stated more clearly the twofold nature of the
Christ.

34. your law here signifies the whole of the Old Testament;
the continued authority of which is thus affirmed.

I said, Ye are gods, cited from Ps. lxxxii. 6, where judges
are called 'gods' and 'sons of the Most High' as reflecting on
earth the Divine work of judgment. Comp. Rom. xiii. 1, 2, 4.
If then judges—'those to whom the word of the Lord came'—
can be called gods, much more should the Christ (Himself the
Word), whom the Father consecrated and sent, be called Son of
God.

36. sanctified, better as *marg.* 'consecrated' to the work
from eternity.

37. If I do not the works of my Father, believe me not.
This is to call to witness the work and character of God as
revealed in the Old Testament. See Introd. p. xxii.

39. They sought again to take him, no longer 'to stone
him.' The last words of Jesus may have softened their wrath.

40-42. Retirement of Jesus to the fords of the Jordan.

And he went away again beyond Jordan into the place 40
where John was at the first baptizing ; and there he
abode. And many came unto him ; and they said, John 41
indeed did no sign : but all things whatsoever John spake
of this man were true. And many believed on him there. 42

11 1-44. The Raising of Lazarus from the dead.

Now a certain man was sick, Lazarus of Bethany, of **11**
the village of Mary and her sister Martha. And it was 2
that Mary which anointed the Lord with ointment, and
wiped his feet with her hair, whose brother Lazarus was
sick. The sisters therefore sent unto him, saying, Lord, 3

---

40. See ch. i. 28.
42. **there**, not only in contrast with the unbelief in Jerusalem,
but also to mark the influence of John in the place where he
baptized.

XI. This is one of the chapters in this Gospel in which
the local and personal notes conclusively point to an eye-witness.
The dramatic animation of the scenes is also characteristic of
St John's style.
1. The raising of Lazarus following on the two other great
miracles is a further sign of the creative power of the Word ;
and a further incentive to the hatred of the Jews, which led to
the condemnation of Jesus.
Bethany, rather less than two miles (see *v.* 13) from Jerusalem,
on the S.E. slope of the mount of Olives, now identified with
El' Azerîyeh, 'The Place of Lazarus.'
Mary and her sister Martha, not named before, but familiar
to St John's disciples from the narrative in Luke x. 38-42. It
is generally recognised that the synoptic Gospels were known to
the readers of St John.
From St Luke we gather that Martha was the elder sister,
and perhaps even the owner of the house : 'she received him
into her house.' Here she acts as hostess, going forth to meet
Jesus, while Mary remains in the house. Nevertheless it is
Mary, whom the Jews come to visit and console, and whom they
accompany to the sepulchre.
2. **which anointed the Lord with ointment,** as narrated in
ch. xii. 3, where see notes and more fully Matt. xxvi. 6-13 ;
Mark xiv. 3-6. There is no good reason for identifying Mary
with the woman that was a sinner, Luke viii. 2.

4 behold, he whom thou lovest is sick. But when Jesus
heard it, he said, This sickness is not unto death, but for
the glory of God, that the Son of God may be glorified
5 thereby.   Now Jesus loved Martha, and her sister, and
6 Lazarus.   When therefore he heard that he was sick, he
abode at that time two days in the place where he was.
7 Then after this he saith to the disciples, Let us go into
8 Judæa again.   The disciples say unto him, Rabbi, the
Jews were but now seeking to stone thee ; and goest thou
9 thither again?   Jesus answered, Are there not twelve
hours in the day?   If a man walk in the day, he
stumbleth not, because he seeth the light of this world.
10 But if a man walk in the night, he stumbleth, because the
11 light is not in him.   These things spake he : and after
this he saith unto them, Our friend Lazarus is fallen
asleep ; but I go, that I may awake him out of sleep.
12 The disciples therefore said unto him, Lord, if he is fallen
13 asleep, he will recover.   Now Jesus had spoken of his
death : but they thought that he spake of taking rest in
14 sleep.   Then Jesus therefore said unto them plainly,
15 Lazarus is dead.   And I am glad for your sakes that
I was not there, to the intent ye may believe ; neverthe-
16 less let us go unto him.   Thomas therefore, who is called
Didymus, said unto his fellow-disciples, Let us also go,
that we may die with him.

---

4.   for the glory of God, see ch. ix. 3.

6.   he abode...two days, no reason is given, but see ch. ii. 4.
The moment of each act is divinely suited to the Divine purpose.

9.   Are there not twelve hours in the day? Comp. ch. ix. 4.
The thought in both cases seems to be that each hour has its
own work, and each work its appointed hour, in which there
will be the light of Divine guidance.   To lose that rightful hour
from fear of danger will be to lose the guiding light.

11.   is fallen asleep, the Greek verb is used of the sleep of
death, Matt. xxvii. 52 ; Acts vii. 60 ; 1 Cor. xv. 18, and elsewhere,
but the words of the disciples shew that this meaning was not
established, or perhaps even usual.

12.   will recover, for 'shall do well,' A.V.

16.   Thomas...who is called Didymus.   The two names bear

So when Jesus came, he found that he had been in the 17
tomb four days already. Now Bethany was nigh unto 18
Jerusalem, about fifteen furlongs off; and many of the 19
Jews had come to Martha and Mary, to console them
concerning their brother. Martha therefore, when she 20
heard that Jesus was coming, went and met him : but
Mary still sat in the house. Martha therefore said unto 21
Jesus, Lord, if thou hadst been here, my brother had not
died. And even now I know that, whatsoever thou shalt 22
ask of God, God will give thee. Jesus saith unto her, 23
Thy brother shall rise again. Martha saith unto him, 24
I know that he shall rise again in the resurrection at the
last day. Jesus said unto her, I am the resurrection, and 25
the life : he that believeth on me, though he die, yet shall
he live : and whosoever liveth and believeth on me shall 26

---

the same meaning, 'twin.' St Thomas's words imply courage,
with a vivid sense of danger.

19. Martha is here named first perhaps as taking the lead in
household management and reception of guests. See *v.* 1, where
Mary is first named.

to console them. Such visits of consolation were customary
during the seven days of mourning for the dead.

20. Note the care with which the Evangelist marks and
contrasts each act of these two women, destined to be typical
characters in the Church of Christ.

22. whatsoever thou shalt ask of God, &c., see *v.* 42, and
vv. 24, 27. The words are interesting as the direct result of the
teaching of Jesus. See ch. xv. 16, where this grace of answered
prayer is transmitted to all true Christians.

25. I am the resurrection, and the life, a further revelation.
The belief in a doctrine is converted into a belief in a Person.
It is characteristic of Christ to raise His disciples in this way to
higher and more mysterious knowledge centred in Himself. He
is Himself the water of life, ch. iv. 14, and the bread of life,
ch. vi. 35. Here He is revealed as the resurrection, because by
the power of Christ (Phil. iii. 10) the dead are raised, and in
Him the believer lives. As He not only gives life and light
but *is* the life and light of the world, so potentially He *is* the
resurrection.

26. whosoever liveth...shall never die. Both Lazarus who
was dead shall live, because he believes, and Martha who

27 never die. Believest thou this? She saith unto him, Yea,
Lord: I have believed that thou art the Christ, the Son
28 of God, *even* he that cometh into the world. And when
she had said this, she went away, and called Mary her
sister secretly, saying, The Master is here, and calleth
29 thee. And she, when she heard it, arose quickly, and
30 went unto him. (Now Jesus was not yet come into the
village, but was still in the place where Martha met
31 him.) The Jews then which were with her in the house,
and were comforting her, when they saw Mary, that she
rose up quickly and went out, followed her, supposing
32 that she was going unto the tomb to weep there. Mary
therefore, when she came where Jesus was, and saw him,
fell down at his feet, saying unto him, Lord, if thou hadst
33 been here, my brother had not died. When Jesus therefore saw her weeping, and the Jews *also* weeping which
came with her, he groaned in the spirit, and was troubled,

---

believed shall never die. Death is not what it seems. In
Christ there is no interruption of life.

Believest thou this? This faith was needed to understand
the significance of the miracle, as a 'sign' of the power of Christ.

27. he that cometh, for 'that should come,' A.V., lit. He
that is coming. Hebr. *Habba*, one of the Messianic titles familiar
to the Jews. He of whom at every epoch it would be true to
say 'he cometh.'

28. secretly, lest the Jews in the house should know of the
presence of Jesus.

32. if thou hadst been here, &c. Mary used the same words
as Martha with much deeper emotion. The sense of grief revives in
the presence of Jesus and she weeps aloud. *Marg.* Gr. *wailing*.

33. groaned in the spirit. In the other passages of the
N.T. where this word occurs it expresses indignation; and the
object of indignation is named (Matt. ix. 30; Mark i. 43, xiv. 5).
Here the object of our Lord's indignation may have been, as
Westcott suggests, the thought of the momentary triumph of
evil, as death, or of Christ's adversary, the devil , or 'the spirit'
may be the direct object of the verb. The meaning would then be
' sternly checked' His spirit, which would humanly shrink from
the coming conflict with death. The same word is used *v.* 38.

was troubled, in sympathy with the sorrow around Him.
Comp. Hebr. iv. 15.

and said, Where have ye laid him? They say unto him, 34
Lord, come and see. Jesus wept. The Jews therefore 35
said, Behold how he loved him! But some of them said, 36
37
Could not this man, which opened the eyes of him that
was blind, have caused that this man also should not die?
Jesus therefore again groaning in himself cometh to the 38
tomb. Now it was a cave, and a stone lay against it.
Jesus saith, Take ye away the stone. Martha, the sister 39
of him that was dead, saith unto him, Lord, by this time
he stinketh: for he hath been *dead* four days. Jesus 40
saith unto her, Said I not unto thee, that, if thou believedst,
thou shouldest see the glory of God? So they took away 41
the stone. And Jesus lifted up his eyes, and said, Father,
I thank thee that thou heardest me. And I knew that 42
thou hearest me always: but because of the multitude
which standeth around I said it, that they may believe
that thou didst send me. And when he had thus spoken, 43
he cried with a loud voice, Lazarus, come forth. He that 44
was dead came forth, bound hand and foot with grave-
clothes; and his face was bound about with a napkin.
Jesus saith unto them, Loose him, and let him go.

---

36. wept, shed tears silently. The verb is found here only
in N.T. and is a different word from that used in *vv.* 31 and 33
to express loud weeping or wailing.

40. the glory of God, the manifestation of His power. See
above *vv.* 25, 26. Comp. Rom. vi. 4, 'Christ was raised
from the dead through the glory of the Father.'

41. I thank thee that thou heardest me. This audible
thanksgiving gives a unique character to this great miracle, and
makes it in a profound sense a sign and proof of union with the
Father. It was a needful preparation for those about to witness
the miracle, shewing them the true character of it (*v.* 42).

43. Lazarus, come forth. The exact words of Jesus in
Aramaic may have been La'âzar tâ lĕbar, the Peshitta version of
this passage, or, La'âzar pôq tâ lĕbar.

44. a napkin, the cloth folded and twisted round the head,
such as is described ch. xx. 7.

The rising again of Lazarus was different from the Resurrection of Jesus Christ as being a return to a corruptible life. It

45, 46. Results of the sign.

45   Many therefore of the Jews, which came to Mary
46 and beheld that which he did, believed on him. But
some of them went away to the Pharisees, and told them
the things which Jesus had done.

47–54. A council of the chief priests and Pharisees about
      Christ.

47   The chief priests therefore and the Pharisees gathered
a council, and said, What do we? for this man doeth
48 many signs. If we let him thus alone, all men will believe
on him : and the Romans will come and take away both
49 our place and our nation. But a certain one of them,
Caiaphas, being high priest that year, said unto them,

---

could not be said of Lazarus 'he dieth no more,' i.e. he is no
longer a dying man, as it could be said of Christ (Rom. vi. 9).

45. which came to Mary. See *vv.* 31, 32.

46. some of them, i.e. some of the Jews, not of those that
came to Mary and believed ; though the latter view is taken by
Origen. In that case the information would be given to the
Pharisees with friendly intention. But this is improbable.

47. therefore, in consequence of this fresh manifestation of
power.

48. the Romans...nation. An armed rising in support of
Jesus would give a sufficient pretext for the Romans to intervene
and destroy the city and the national existence of the Jews. No
groundless fear, for this eventually came to pass.

49. Caiaphas, being high priest. Joseph Caiaphas was
appointed high priest by the Procurator Valerius Gratus (pre-
decessor of Pontius Pilate) in A.D. 26 and was deposed A.D. 38.
He was son-in-law to Annas, who had been high priest from
B.C. 7–15, and still retained the title and dignity in the estima-
tion of the people, who did not recognise his deposition ; comp.
Luke iii. 2; Acts iv. 6. Caiaphas from the moment the death of
Jesus was determined upon took the lead in bringing it about.
The Pharisees do not appear as actively hostile in the events of
the Passion.

that year, that great year in the world's history, when all types
were fulfilled, and the redemption of man was accomplished. It
is not of course implied that the high priesthood was an annual
office.

Ye know nothing at all, nor do ye take account that it is 50
expedient for you that one man should die for the people,
and that the whole nation perish not. Now this he said 51
not of himself : but being high priest that year, he
prophesied that Jesus should die for the nation ; and not 52
for the nation only, but that he might also gather together
into one the children of God that are scattered abroad.
So from that day forth they took counsel that they might 53
put him to death.

Jesus therefore walked no more openly among the Jews, 54
but departed thence into the country near to the
wilderness, into a city called Ephraim ; and there he
tarried with the disciples.

PART III. Passiontide. **11** 55—**19** 41.

55-57. Approach of the Passover—Orders to betray Jesus.

Now the passover of the Jews was at hand: and many 55

Ye know nothing at all, a contemptuous rejection of the
arguments of the other side. Bp Lightfoot remarks that this
scornful speech accords with the Sadducean character for rude-
ness as drawn by Josephus, *Bell. Jud.* II. viii. 14.

50. it is expedient, &c., regardless of all justice Caiaphas
argued that the death of Jesus was expedient to avoid a tumult
and its consequences. The phrase he employs is a well-known
Jewish adage (Edersheim).

51. A note by St John.

he prophesied, unconsciously he uttered a profound truth
involving the doctrine of the Atonement.

52. and not for the nation only. The Evangelist, living at
a time when the mystery of the Gospel to the Gentiles had been
made known, notes the extension of the Atonement to other
nations besides the Jews; comp. Acts ii. 39.

53. from that day forth. The advice of Caiaphas was
adopted.

54. therefore, because His hour had not yet come.

a city called Ephraim, possibly the modern El-Taiyibeh; if so,
a town of Judæa on the borders of Samaria, G. A. Smith, *Geog.* &c.
p. 325. It was probably not far from Bethel, Lightfoot, *Bib.
Essays,* pp. 27 and 177.

55. Now the passover of the Jews, in contrast with the

went up to Jerusalem out of the country before the pass-
56 over, to purify themselves.   They sought therefore for
Jesus, and spake one with another, as they stood in the
temple, What think ye? That he will not come to the
57 feast?   Now the chief priests and the Pharisees had given
commandment, that, if any man knew where he was, he
should shew it, that they might take him.

> **12** 1–8.   The Supper at Bethany.   Matthew xxvi. 6–13.
> Mark xiv. 3–9.   The incident in Luke vii. 36–40, some-
> times cited as parallel, belongs to a different occasion.   The
> accidents alone correspond.

12 Jesus therefore six days before the passover came to
Bethany, where Lazarus was, whom Jesus raised from the
2 dead.   So they made him a supper there: and Martha

Christian passover, to which St John's readers had become
accustomed, comp. 1 Cor. v. 7.
   to purify themselves, comp. 2 Chron. xxx. 17, 18, and
ch. xviii. 28, and Joseph. *B. J.* v. iii. 1, where there is an account
of Jews treacherously introduced into the Temple, 'the greater
part of whom were not purified.'

   XII. 1.   six days before the passover. If this be reckoned from
Friday, Nisan 14, the arrival at Bethany must be placed on
Saturday, Nisan 8 (in the evening when the Sabbath was over).
   came to Bethany. By comparing this account with the
synoptics we learn that Jesus had left Ephraim (xi. 54) and
had gone to Jericho, whence He would make the ascent to
Jerusalem with the caravan of pilgrims.
   whom Jesus raised from the dead, omit 'which had been
dead' A.V.
   2.   they made him a supper, Matt. xxvi. 6 f. and Mk xiv. 3 f.
add 'in the house of Simon the leper.'   It is not however stated
that Simon was the host or related to Martha and Mary, or that
he was present at the feast (if he was still a leper he could not
have sat at meat with the rest).   The facts given are that 'they
made him a feast,' that Lazarus was there as a guest, and that
Martha took the chief place in ministering.   It has been suggested
that the feast was given in honour of Jesus by the inhabitants of
Bethany.   In that case the house of Simon the leper may have
been untenanted or at any rate placed at their disposal for the
feast.

served ; but Lazarus was one of them that sat at meat
with him. Mary therefore took a pound of ointment of 3
spikenard, very precious, and anointed the feet of Jesus,
and wiped his feet with her hair : and the house was filled
with the odour of the ointment. But Judas Iscariot, one 4
of his disciples, which should betray him, saith, Why 5
was not this ointment sold for three hundred pence, and
given to the poor ? Now this he said, not because he cared 6
for the poor ; but because he was a thief, and having the bag

---

3. a pound of ointment of spikenard, very precious, 'an
alabaster cruse (or flask, *marg.*) of exceeding precious ointment'
(lit. myrrh); Matt. 'an alabaster cruse of spikenard very costly';
Mark ; where see *margin* as to the rare Greek word (πιστικῆς)
there used. Spikenard, an exclusively Indian product, was
imported into Palestine at a very early period (Tristram, *Nat.
Hist. of the Bible*); comp. Cant. i. 12, 'while the king sat at his
table my spikenard sent forth its fragrance.'

the feet of Jesus, Matt. and Mk have 'poured it over his
head.' Such discrepancy has been needlessly pressed. It is
possible that both head and feet were anointed.

The name of Mary is not mentioned in the synoptics.

the house was filled...ointment. This point of vivid remembrance is found in this Gospel only. On the other hand St John
omits 'this shall be done for a memorial of her' or for her
memorial. The 'fragrance' suggests the memorial sacrifice, see
Phil. iv. 18, 'an odour of a sweet smell, a sacrifice acceptable,
well-pleasing to God.' Comp. Eph. v. 2.

4. Judas Iscariot...saith. In Matt. the objection is made by
'the disciples,' in Mark it is said 'some' had indignation &c.

5. three hundred pence, if a penny or *denarius* be taken as
a day's wage (see Matt. xx. 2) the three hundred pence would be
equivalent to nearly a year's income. It was possibly the whole
of her wealth.

The two acts of Mary and Judas are impressively contrasted
by their juxtaposition.

6. having the bag, or better as *marg.* 'box.' (The word is
used of the money chest in the Temple, 2 Kings xii. 9); it
contained the common fund for the support of Jesus and His
Apostles.

A. Wright (*Synoptics*, p. 31) conjectures that 'although Iscariot
stands last in all the lists, it may be that he had once been first.
Else he had not been entrusted with the bag.' The first became
last, and the last first. There is, however, little to support this
dramatic suggestion.

7 took away what was put therein. Jesus therefore said,
Suffer her to keep it against the day of my burying.

8 For the poor ye have always with you ; but me ye have
not always.

9-11. Popular interest in Jesus and in Lazarus.

9   The common people therefore of the Jews learned that

took away what was put therein, for 'bare what was put
therein,' A.V., which agrees with the *marg.* 'carried.' The
R.V. is however justified by the usage of the word, which has
been recently confirmed by *papyri* inscriptions. (*Expositor,*
Dec. 1903.)

7. Suffer her to keep it, &c., see *marg.*, 'Let her alone, it was
that she might keep it,' &c. If the rendering of R.V. be followed
the meaning must be 'let her keep it—i.e. what remains of the
precious ointment against the day of my burying.'   Either
rendering requires the inference that Mary had not poured out
the whole of the precious ointment. But this inference is not
warranted by the words of the Evangelists (note the strong
compound κατέχεεν for 'poured' in the synoptics). Moreover
this rendering disturbs the meaning of our Lord's words, by
which this good and beautiful work of Mary is regarded as an
anticipation of His burying, which by faith she foresaw. It is
this foresight of faith that gives the character to her act.

The reading followed by A.V. 'she hath kept it for my burial,'
though found in none of the uncial MSS. except one, viz. 19,
gives a better sense, and may be right. In any case the meaning is
that this good and beautiful act of Mary is in view of the burial
of Jesus, which by faith she foresaw.

It has been conjectured that the precious ointment was brought
for the entombment of Lazarus, and that it might have been sold,
but that Mary reserved it for the burial of Jesus. Jesus implies
that she *is* using it now for His burial.

8. the poor ye have always with you, &c.   These are
important words. The argument of Judas had an appearance
of charity and wisdom ; but, if unwisely pressed, it would hinder
many works of Christian devotion, which seems on the surface
to be a wasting of precious things.   Judas failed to see the
deeper meaning of Mary's act, which had a purpose and a use
approved by Jesus.

9. The common people, for 'much people' A.V.   It was
the common people on whom the Pharisees and chief priests
depended for support, and their defection therefore was a serious
hindrance to the plot against Jesus. Although Bethany was more
than a Sabbath day's journey from Jerusalem it was regarded by
the Rabbinical rules as forming part of the city.

he was there : and they came, not for Jesus' sake only,
but that they might see Lazarus also, whom he had raised
from the dead. But the chief priests took counsel that 10
they might put Lazarus also to death ; because that by 11
reason of him many of the Jews went away, and believed
on Jesus.

12–19. The Triumph of Palm Sunday. Matthew xxi. 1–11.
    Mark xi. 1–11. Luke xix. 29–44.

On the morrow a great multitude that had come to the 12
feast, when they heard that Jesus was coming to Jerusalem, took the branches of the palm trees, and went forth 13
to meet him, and cried out, Hosanna : Blessed *is* he that
cometh in the name of the Lord, even the King of Israel.
And Jesus, having found a young ass, sat thereon ; as it 14
is written, Fear not, daughter of Zion : behold, thy King 15

---

12. On the morrow, the first day of the week, our Palm
Sunday.
    that Jesus was coming to Jerusalem. For once Jesus yielded
to the enthusiasm of His disciples. It was necessary that once
He should be recognised as King of Israel.
    13. went forth to meet him, the procession from Bethany was
met by one coming from Jerusalem across the valley of Kidron.
    Hosanna (*Heb.* **hosiah-na**) 'save I pray'; *na* is a particle
of entreaty added to imperatives. This and the following words
are cited from Ps. cxviii. 25, 26. It was the last Psalm of the
Hallel and was written probably either for the dedication of the
second Temple or for the laying of the foundation-stone. These
verses were sung in procession round the altar at the Feast of
Tabernacles and on other joyous occasions.
    he that cometh, see ch. xi. 27.
    14. having found a young ass. The circumstances are
narrated at length in the synoptic Gospels. The ass is a much
nobler animal in the East than in Northern climates, where it
degenerates. White asses were in special repute and were used
to carry distinguished persons (Judges v. 10, x. 4, xii. 14).
    15. Fear not, daughter of Zion, &c. Cited from Zech. ix. 9.
This and the following chapter describe the triumph of Zion over
the world powers, and the deliverance and peace of Israel, ' No
oppressor shall pass through them any more,' *v.* 8. The immediate context shews that the ass is a symbol of peace as
opposed to the war-chariot and the horse, *v.* 10.

16 cometh, sitting on an ass's colt. These things understood not his disciples at the first : but when Jesus was glorified, then remembered they that these things were written of
17 him, and that they had done these things unto him. The multitude therefore that was with him when he called Lazarus out of the tomb, and raised him from the dead,
18 bare witness. For this cause also the multitude went and met him, for that they heard that he had done this sign.
19 The Pharisees therefore said among themselves, Behold how ye prevail nothing : lo, the world is gone after him.

20–36 a. The Greeks desire to see Jesus, 20–22. Teaching of Jesus in the Temple for the last time, 23–36 a.

20 Now there were certain Greeks among those that went
21 up to worship at the feast : these therefore came to Philip,

---

16. These things understood not his disciples at the first. Another of the Evangelist's reflexions on the acts or words of our Lord, which are a distinguishing mark of this Gospel. Comp. xiii. 7.

17. The multitude therefore that was with him, &c. The eye-witnesses of this verse are distinguished from those dwellers in Jerusalem alluded to in v. 12, who had only heard the report of the miracle.

17–19. St John here notes the twofold effect of the resurrection of Lazarus,—on the one hand a rapidly growing belief in Jesus among the common people, on the other a fixed determination on the part of the Pharisees to put Him to death.

20–36. It is uncertain on which day this incident took place. But its importance in the Evangelist's eyes is indicated by its position in the narrative. It is with him the last recorded act before the Passion, to which it bears a close relation. The supreme value of this incident consists partly in that relation, and partly in its reference to the incoming of the Gentiles.

20. Greeks, i.e. Greek proselytes, foreigners who spoke the Greek language and had attached themselves to the Jewish religion ; to be distinguished from Hellenists, or Greek-speaking Jews. Many of the proselytes became Christians, of whom the first named is Nicolas, a proselyte of Antioch, Acts vi. 5. S. Luke was also probably a proselyte. Both he and Nicolas may have been present on this occasion.

among those that went up. More accurately, 'of the number of those who went up, there were some Greeks,' &c.

21. Philip. Both his Greek name and his home in Galilee

which was of Bethsaida of Galilee, and asked him, saying,
Sir, we would see Jesus. Philip cometh and telleth Andrew: 22
Andrew cometh, and Philip, and they tell Jesus. And 23
Jesus answereth them, saying, The hour is come, that the
Son of man should be glorified. Verily, verily, I say unto 24
you, Except a grain of wheat fall into the earth and die,
it abideth by itself alone; but if it die, it beareth much
fruit. He that loveth his life loseth it; and he that hateth 25
his life in this world shall keep it unto life eternal. If any 26
man serve me, let him follow me; and where I am, there
shall also my servant be: if any man serve me, him will
the Father honour. Now is my soul troubled; and what 27

---

would attract these Greek-speaking strangers. The same two
reasons would apply to Andrew. Philip seeks Andrew to share
the responsibility of this new departure (comp. Matt. viii. 11),
partly, perhaps, because he belongs to the first group of four
Apostles, partly because it seems to have been his privilege to
bring people to Jesus, see chs. i. 42, vi. 8, 9.

would see Jesus, i.e. converse with Him, and know Him. We
use the word 'see' in the same sense.

23. should be glorified. The full glory or manifestation of
Jesus was by the death on the Cross. The death and self-
sacrifice as explained in *vv.* 24 and 25 are necessary conditions
of eternal life.

24. fall into the earth and die, &c. This is not only a
parable or symbol of death as a condition of life; it is the
revelation of a law of nature in its highest sense. St Paul
expands this great thought, 1 Cor. xv. 36 foll.

25. He that loveth his life loseth it. See Matt. x. 39.
The sacrifice of the lower life and instincts is needed in order to
gain the higher life.

26. where I am, there shall also my servant be, the faithful
servant who follows his Master through suffering and death shall
be ever with his Lord. 'If we endure we shall also reign
with him,' 2 Tim. ii. 12. It has been noted that the Greek
view of life was different, the whole tendency of which was to
perfect the enjoyment of human life. Jesus reveals the secret of
the Cross and its wonderful attractiveness.

27. Now is my soul troubled, as in the Garden of Gethsemane, Luke xxii. 44; Hebr. v. 7.

what shall I say? The human will hesitates; for the choice
is still open (ch. x. 18) to lay down the life or 'save' it.

shall I say? Father, save me from this hour. But for this
28 cause came I unto this hour. Father, glorify thy name.
There came therefore a voice out of heaven, *saying*, I
29 have both glorified it, and will glorify it again. The
multitude therefore, that stood by, and heard it, said that
it had thundered: others said, An angel hath spoken to
30 him. Jesus answered and said, This voice hath not come
31 for my sake, but for your sakes. Now is the judgement
of this world: now shall the prince of this world be cast
32 out. And I, if I be lifted up from the earth, will draw all
33 men unto myself. But this he said, signifying by what
34 manner of death he should die. The multitude therefore

---

save me from this hour. Some editors make this interroga-
tive. It is better taken as a prayer, and so may be compared
with the prayer at Gethsemane, 'If it be thy will let this cup
pass from me.' See however *margin*. 'Save me from this hour,'
'bring My soul in safety through this hour of temptation; make
Me pass safely through it'; not, 'deliver Me from entering into
it' (Westcott).

for this cause, i.e. to suffer, in order to reign; to die, in order
to save mankind.

28. a voice out of heaven. See Matt. iii. 17 and parallels.

31. Now is the judgement of this world. The crucifixion
of Jesus is the condemnation of the world which acquiesces in it.
At all times the Cross has been a test by which men are judged;
condemned or saved. By the Cross also the power of Satan is
overthrown. Ever since Calvary Christ has literally been King,
the dominant force in the world; comp. Col. ii. 15; 2 Cor. v. 17.
In a true sense He was 'glorified' by the Cross.

32. And I, if I be lifted up from the earth, &c. The
reference seems to be both to the Crucifixion and to the Ascension
of our Lord. (1) The 'lifting up' of the Crucifixion taught
men the great and abiding lesson that sacrifice, and not selfishness,
is the highest ideal of the moral life; see Matt. x. 38, xvi. 24
and parallels. (2) It was not till after the Ascension that the
full meaning, and hence the attractiveness, of the Cross of Christ
was manifested; see 1 Cor. ii. 2.

33. See ch. xviii. 32, and for other 'notes' of the Evangelist,
comp. ch. vii. 39, xviii. 9, xix. 36, xxi. 19. 'Such notes convey
the impression of a writer looking back on the events from
a distance of time' (Westcott, *St John*, p. 36).

34. The people again compare their theory of the Christ
with the facts as they conceive them. The answer of Jesus is

answered him, We have heard out of the law that the
Christ abideth for ever: and how sayest thou, The Son of
man must be lifted up? who is this Son of man? Jesus 35
therefore said unto them, Yet a little while is the light
among you. Walk while ye have the light, that darkness
overtake you not: and he that walketh in the darkness
knoweth not whither he goeth. While ye have the light, 36
believe on the light, that ye may become sons of light.

36 b–50. The final judgment on the result of our Lord's
ministry; (a) by the Evangelist, 37–43; (b) by Christ
Himself, 44–50.

These things spake Jesus, and he departed and hid
himself from them. But though he had done so many 37
signs before them, yet they believed not on him: that 38
the word of Isaiah the prophet might be fulfilled, which
he spake,

Lord, who hath believed our report?

And to whom hath the arm of the Lord been revealed?

---

contained in *vv.* 35, 36. Belief 'on the light' will lead to that
knowledge and all other knowledge. If they are sons of light,
illuminated with Divine intelligence, they will know in what way
'Christ abideth for ever,' and in what manner He reigns.

Son of man, a title used by Jesus of Himself, never by others
of Him, except by St Stephen, Acts vii. 56. 'It is a title based
on an infinite sense of brotherhood with feeling and suffering
humanity' (Prof. Sanday). Comp. ch. i. 51.

36. sons of light. Comp. Ephes. v. 3, 'Walk as children
of light.'

hid himself from them. The moment of enlightenment is
past.

37. though he had done so many signs. In the full
description of those last 'signs' (chs. v., ix.–xii.), the Evangelist
shews how clearly the power of God in Christ was manifested in
this way.

38. Lord, who hath believed our report? Is. liii. 1, also
cited Rom. x. 16. In Isaiah the reference is to 'the servant of
the Lord,' who 'willingly accepted the vast but inevitable
sufferings which lay on his road to glory' (Cheyne), and to the
share of the Gentiles in the Messiah's victory. It is a passage
therefore which bears closely on our Lord's words just uttered,

39 For this cause they could not believe, for that Isaiah
   said again,

40 　He hath blinded their eyes, and he hardened their
   　　heart;

   　Lest they should see with their eyes, and perceive with
   　　their heart,

   　And should turn,

   　And I should heal them.

41 These things said Isaiah, because he saw his glory;
42 and he spake of him. Nevertheless even of the rulers
   many believed on him; but because of the Pharisees they
   did not confess *it*, lest they should be put out of the
43 synagogue: for they loved the glory of men more than
   the glory of God.

44 　And Jesus cried and said, He that believeth on me,
45 believeth not on me, but on him that sent me. And he
46 that beholdeth me beholdeth him that sent me. I am

---

and on the whole of His ministry. Jesus Christ was rejected by
this generation, as the prophetic picture of Him was rejected by
the Jews of the Captivity.

40. He hath blinded their eyes, &c. Is. vi. 10, where the
prophet is told of the refusal of Israel to accept his ministry.
Jesus Himself quotes the words in the same sense, Matt. xiii.
14, 15.

41. because he saw his glory. For 'when he saw his glory,'
A.V.; see Is. vi. 1 foll., where the appearance of the King, 'the
Lord of hosts,' is described, and the mission of the prophet. The
inference is that to see the glory of God is to see the glory of
Christ, who is the 'Word,' God revealed in the flesh. So belief
in Christ is belief in God, see below *vv.* 44, 45. He that hath
seen God hath seen Christ.

42. even of the rulers many believed on him. Comp. Acts
vi. 7, 'A great company of priests were obedient unto the
faith.' As yet however the rulers had not the courage of their
belief—a contrast to the blind man who was cured, ch. ix.

44. cried and said, not on one special occasion but on many.
Each word in the passage which follows has been already spoken.
It is a summary and restatement of great truths in the teaching
of Jesus: His oneness with the Father—His Mission as the light
of the world—The responsibility for rejection.

come a light into the world, that whosoever believeth on
me may not abide in the darkness. And if any man 47
hear my sayings, and keep them not, I judge him not:
for I came not to judge the world, but to save the world.
He that rejecteth me, and receiveth not my sayings, hath 48
one that judgeth him: the word that I spake, the same
shall judge him in the last day. For I spake not from 49
myself; but the Father which sent me, he hath given me
a commandment, what I should say, and what I should
speak. And I know that his commandment is life eternal: 50
the things therefore which I speak, even as the Father
hath said unto me, so I speak.

13 1—17 26. The Last Supper and discourses thereat.   1-20
    Jesus washes His disciples' feet; and teaches humility.

Now before the feast of the passover, Jesus knowing **13**
that his hour was come that he should depart out of
this world unto the Father, having loved his own which
were in the world, he loved them unto the end. And 2

---

47. I judge him not. Christ as redeemer of the world does
not judge, but hereafter His words will judge those who rejected
them.
50. his commandment is life eternal. Eternal life consists
not in philosophy or science, but in obedience to the will of God
revealed in Christ; 'whom truly to know is eternal life.'

XIII. The section from ch. xiii.—xvii. 26 is in strong contrast
with the preceding section, where Jesus is in conflict with the
unbelief and hostility of the Jews. Here He manifests His love
to His disciples, strengthens their faith, and intercedes for them.
    The dispute as to who should be greatest recorded by the
synoptists took place before the Supper; with this is closely
connected the feet-washing narrated by St John alone.
1. knowing that his hour was come, see chs. ii. 6, vii. 30,
viii. 20, xii. 23. The expression shews that each act in our
Lord's life was divinely ordered, and was in His knowledge and
in His will.
unto the end. The reading in *marg.* 'to the uttermost' is
preferable.
    Bishop Westcott places the distribution of the Bread at this
point—before *v.* 2—and the distribution of the Cup after *v.* 32.

during supper, the devil having already put into the heart of
3 Judas Iscariot, Simon's *son*, to betray him, *Jesus*, knowing
that the Father had given all things into his hands, and
4 that he came forth from God, and goeth unto God, riseth
from supper, and layeth aside his garments; and he took
5 a towel, and girded himself. Then he poureth water into
the bason, and began to wash the disciples' feet, and to
6 wipe them with the towel wherewith he was girded. So
he cometh to Simon Peter. He saith unto him, Lord,
7 dost thou wash my feet? Jesus answered and said unto
him, What I do thou knowest not now; but thou shalt
8 understand hereafter. Peter saith unto him, Thou shalt
never wash my feet. Jesus answered him, If I wash thee

---

2. during supper, for 'supper being ended,' A.V. **the
devil having already**, &c., for 'the devil having now,' &c., A.V.
Both these corrections are important. The first shews that the
feet-washing took place in the course of the paschal meal; the
second that Judas had formed his plans for betrayal before the
Last Supper. The treachery of Judas is named at the commencement of the narrative in order that the allusions in *vv.* 10,
18, 21 should be understood.

3. knowing, i.e. because He knew, because of His greatness,
of His union with the Father, He humbles Himself. Comp.
Phil. ii. 6–8, 'who being in the form of God...humbled himself,
becoming obedient even unto death, yea, the death of the cross,'
and Ps. xviii. 35, 'Thy condescension hath made me great.'
had given all things into his hands. See Matt. xi. 27,
xxviii. 18, and ch. xvii. 2.

4. took a towel, the dress of a slave : 'taking the form of a
servant,' Phil. ii. 7. Comp. 1 Peter v. 5, 'all of you gird yourselves with humility, to serve one another,' where there is
probably a reference to this incident, which would always be
vividly present to St Peter's mind.

5. the bason, which would be in the room (not '*a* bason,'
A.V.).

6. dost thou wash my feet ? To deprecate this service was
to fail to comprehend the spirit of Christ, and the revelation of
humility and love. This humility of St Peter had its source in
pride.

7. understand, for 'know,' A.V. Time threw light on many
words and acts of Jesus, not understood at first.

not, thou hast no part with me. Simon Peter saith unto 9
him, Lord, not my feet only, but also my hands and my
head. Jesus saith to him, He that is bathed needeth not 10
save to wash his feet, but is clean every whit: and ye
are clean, but not all. For he knew him that should 11
betray him; therefore said he, Ye are not all clean.

So when he had washed their feet, and taken his 12
garments, and sat down again, he said unto them, Know
ye what I have done to you? Ye call me, Master, and, 13
Lord: and ye say well; for so I am. If I then, the Lord 14
and the Master, have washed your feet, ye also ought
to wash one another's feet. For I have given you an 15
example, that ye also should do as I have done to you.
Verily, verily, I say unto you, A servant is not greater 16

---

8. hast no part with me, unless you submit to this act and
enter into the meaning of it, you can have no share in my
discipleship.

9. not my feet only, &c. This sudden change of mood is
characteristic of St Peter. Comp. the change from over-con-
fidence to fear, Matt. xiv. 30, from devotion to denial, *infra*
v. 38, xxvi. 58, 69, from courage to flight, ch. xviii. 10, Matt.
xxvi. 56.

10. He that is bathed (better than 'washed,' A.V.). There
is probably a reference to baptism (comp. 1 Cor. vi. 11; Titus
iii. 5). There is no need that that should be repeated; but just
as washing the feet was needed daily, so the spirit of humility,
now symbolised by it, must always be present in the Christian
life.

not all, said partly, perhaps, to give Judas one more chance
for repentance, partly to shew His other disciples that He fore-
knew all.

11. knew him that should betray him, for 'knew who
should betray,' A.V., better still perhaps, 'knew him that was
betraying him.' He knew the heart of Judas. The treachery
had begun.

12. Know ye, rather 'understand,' as the same word is
translated *v.* 7.

14. the Lord and the Master (for 'your Lord and Master,'
A.V.).

15. an example, a pattern to be imitated in many other
ways and in different circumstances.

16. See Matt. x. 24.

than his lord; neither one that is sent greater than he
17 that sent him.   If ye know these things, blessed are ye if
18 ye do them.   I speak not of you all: I know whom I have
chosen: but that the scripture may be fulfilled, He that
19 eateth my bread lifted up his heel against me.   From
henceforth I tell you before it come to pass, that, when it
20 is come to pass, ye may believe that I am *he*.   Verily,
verily, I say unto you, He that receiveth whomsoever I
send receiveth me; and he that receiveth me receiveth
him that sent me.

21-30.   Judas, designated as traitor, departs.

21   When Jesus had thus said, he was troubled in the spirit,
and testified, and said, Verily, verily, I say unto you, that
22 one of you shall betray me.   The disciples looked one
23 on another, doubting of whom he spake.   There was at
the table reclining in Jesus' bosom one of his disciples,
24 whom Jesus loved.   Simon Peter therefore beckoneth to

---

17.   blessed, not only in the consciousness of an act of charity,
but also because he who thus acts is most Christ-like, and
greatest in the kingdom of heaven.

18.   my bread, for 'bread with me,' A.V.   See Ps. xli. 9.
The most cruel treachery is the 'treachery of a friend.   This was
the Psalmist's sorrow, and is Christ's also, see *v.* 26.

19.   See *v.* 11.

20.   This verse explains the last words of the preceding verse,
and sets forth the surprising dignity of the Lord and the Master.

21.   was troubled in the spirit, in horror, we may believe,
at the awful crime contemplated by Judas.

23.   reclining in Jesus' bosom.   As a rule at an ancient
banquet there were three couches arranged on three sides of a
square (*triclinium*).   The guests reclined, the left elbow resting
on a cushion.   John being next to Jesus is said to recline in His
bosom.   When he 'leant back,' *v.* 23, he would be in close
contact with Jesus, and could whisper to Him.

one of his disciples, whom Jesus loved; that this was John is
certain from the fact that he must have been one of the three most
favoured by our Lord.   But this passage proves that it was not
Peter, nor could it have been James, to whom the words spoken
of the disciple 'whom Jesus loved,' ch. xxi. 20, would not have
been applicable.   It follows then that it is St John who is thus
described.

him, and saith unto him, Tell *us* who it is of whom he
speaketh. He leaning back, as he was, on Jesus' breast 25
saith unto him, Lord, who is it? Jesus therefore answer- 26
eth, He it is, for whom I shall dip the sop, and give it
him. So when he had dipped the sop, he taketh and
giveth it to Judas, *the son* of Simon Iscariot. And after 27
the sop, then entered Satan into him. Jesus therefore
saith unto him, That thou doest, do quickly. Now no 28
man at the table knew for what intent he spake this unto
him. For some thought, because Judas had the bag, that 29
Jesus said unto him, Buy what things we have need of for
the feast; or, that he should give something to the poor.
He then having received the sop went out straightway: 30
and it was night.

31–35. The New Commandment.

When therefore he was gone out, Jesus saith, Now is 31
the Son of man glorified, and God is glorified in him;

---

24. **Tell us who it is**, &c., for 'that he should ask,' &c., A.V.
25. **leaning back, as he was, on Jesus' breast**, for 'lying on
Jesus' breast,' A.V. The R.V. makes the picture more vivid.
26. **He it is**, &c. These words were probably whispered, so
that the others could not hear; see *v.* 28. This was the tragic
moment selected by Leonardo da Vinci for his immortal picture
of the Last Supper. According to St Matthew xxvi. 23 foll. the
disciples openly asked: 'Is it I?' and Jesus said to Judas
(probably in a low voice) 'Thou hast said.'
dip the sop. It is still customary in the East for the host to
take a choice portion from the dish and present it to a favoured
guest. Here 'the sop' is a piece of bread dipped in the sauce.
This was perhaps a last call to repentance for Judas.
Judas, the son of Simon Iscariot, for 'Judas Iscariot the son
of Simon,' A.V. Both father and son had the name of their
native place, Kerioth. Iscariot=man (*ish*) of Kerioth.
27. **Satan,** named here only in this Gospel.
29. **because Judas had the bag.** See ch. xii. 6.
30. **it was night,** an impressive note—the hour suited the
dark deed. It was probably after the departure of Judas that
the institution of the Eucharist took place. See Matt. xxvi.
26–29; Mk xiv. 22–25; Luke xxii. 19, 20.
31. **Now is the Son of man glorified,** from this moment the

32 and God shall glorify him in himself, and straightway
33 shall he glorify him. Little children, yet a little while
I am with you. Ye shall seek me: and as I said unto the
Jews, Whither I go, ye cannot come; so now I say unto
34 you. A new commandment I give unto you, that ye love
one another; even as I have loved you, that ye also love
35 one another. By this shall all men know that ye are my
disciples, if ye have love one to another.

36–38. The presumption of Peter rebuked.

36 Simon Peter saith unto him, Lord, whither goest thou?
Jesus answered, Whither I go, thou canst not follow me

Passion begins through which, by the humiliation and above all
by the self-sacrifice of it, Jesus was glorified.

32. The words 'If God be glorified in him,' A.V., are omitted
in R.V. God is glorified as manifested by the self-sacrifice of
Christ; and shall glorify Christ by taking Him to Himself in
union with the Godhead.

33. Little children. As a consequence of the glory of Christ
He must leave His disciples for a time. In so doing He uses
the tender word, here only in this Gospel, 'little children.' His
disciples have become like little children, through the teaching
of humility. St John borrows this affectionate address, using it
many times in his first Epistle.

34. A new commandment, *mandatum novum.* This was
the 'command' literally obeyed on Maundy Thursday (*dies
mandati*). For its observance in a Benedictine monastery see
Dean Church's *Anselm*, pp. 49–51. Love henceforth becomes
the watchword and essence of the Christian life. For love to
grow cold is for Christianity to lose its enthusiasm. The love
of that faithful company with their common work, and sufferings
in common, was to be the model of the Christian Society:

> 'Companionship in toil or sorrow
> Makes every man a brother,
> Till we have worked and wept together
> We do not know each other.' (E. ELLIOTT.)

So the *agapè* or love feast becomes the distinguishing mark of
Christians.

36. whither goest thou? The intense desire of His disciples
to know what the Master meant breaks out in the words of
St Peter.

now; but thou shalt follow afterwards. Peter saith unto 37
him, Lord, why cannot I follow thee even now? I will
lay down my life for thee. Jesus answereth, Wilt thou 38
lay down thy life for me? Verily, verily, I say unto thee,
The cock shall not crow, till thou hast denied me thrice.

---

37. I will lay down my life for thee. Comp. 'greater love
hath no man than this that he lay down his life for his friend,'
xv. 13. St Peter aspires to this height of love.

38. The Master still does not explain. Nor does He deny
that St Peter will lay down his life for Him. Only He shews
that there will first be failure.

Additional Note.

The Paschal meal. It is impossible within the limits of these
notes to enter fully into the controversy respecting the character
of the Paschal meal, and the day and hour when Christ partook
of it with His disciples. But the following solution is suggested
as the most probable.

The 14th of Nisan commenced on the evening of the day
which we should call the 13th Nisan[1]. We believe then that the
Last Supper or Paschal meal took place after sunset on the
13th, that is, strictly speaking, on the commencement of the
14th Nisan, which was a Friday, the 'Preparation' before the
Passover, which this year fell on a Sabbath-day. The arrest
took place the same night and the trials the next morning; and
the Crucifixion also was carried out on the 14th Nisan from
9 a.m. to 3 p.m. (Mark xv. 25, 'It was the third hour, and they
crucified him'), when lambs were being sacrificed in the Temple
courts in view of the regular Passover meal on the 15th Nisan,
i.e. after sunset on the 14th.

According to this view the 'Last Supper' was not the regular
Paschal meal, but one of a Paschal character eaten beforehand
owing to the necessity of the case. For confirmation of this
see 1 Cor. xi. 23, where St Paul dates the institution of the
Lord's Supper not 'on the night of the Passover,' but 'on the
night when he was betrayed'; and in 1 Cor. xi. 23 he speaks
of 'Christ our Passover' being sacrificed, thus referring the
Crucifixion to the time described above.

The difficulty in maintaining the above account lies in the
assertion of the Synoptists that it was on 'the first day of
unleavened bread, when they sacrificed the Passover' that the
disciples asked where the Passover was to be eaten, whereas

---

[1] On the feast of unleavened bread, it being the fourteenth of the month
Xanthicus (Nisan). Josephus, *B. J.* v. iii. 1.

14 1-4. The House of many mansions.

14 Let not your heart be troubled : ye believe in God,
2 believe also in me. In my Father's house are many
mansions ; if it were not so, I would have told you ; for
3 I go to prepare a place for you. And if I go and prepare
a place for you, I come again, and will receive you unto
4 myself; that where I am, *there* ye may be also. And
whither I go, ye know the way.

St John says distinctly that the Supper was eaten 'before the
feast of the passover' (xiii. 1). Various explanations of this
discrepancy have been given, but none can be thought entirely
satisfactory. The most probable solution is that as all leaven
had to be removed before noon or even sooner on the 14th, that
day was sometimes regarded as the first day of unleavened bread
—a suggestion which finds confirmation in Josephus, *B. J.* v.
iii. 1. When then the disciples enquire about preparing for the
Passover on the *next* day, they are told in effect to make ready
at once. St John calls the meal 'a supper,' but it was certainly
of a Paschal character.

But however the discrepancy may be explained, the preference
must be given to St John's narrative, and notes of time. The
typical character of the death of Christ is greatly enhanced if
it synchronised with the Paschal sacrifice then being celebrated
in the Temple Courts.

XIV. 1-4. These verses are an answer to the question so
impetuously pressed by St Peter. It would have been a better
division if the chapter had begun at *v.* 31 or 36 of ch. xiii.
1. ye believe in God, believe also in me. Absolute trust in
God gave the assurance of eternal life to believers under the old
covenant (see Pss. xvi. 11, xvii. 15; Is. xxvi. 19; Dan. xii. 2);
the same trust deepened by the revelation in Christ gives the
same assurance now.
2. many mansions, or 'abiding places,' *marg.* The image
is taken either (1) from a large Oriental palace, in which
numerous courtiers and attendants would lodge; or (2) from
the *stationes* or resting-places on a road. The latter meaning
however is less applicable here.
4. ye know the way, because Christ Himself is the way.
But this the disciples do not understand until Jesus explains.

5, 6. Christ the Way.

Thomas saith unto him, Lord, we know not whither thou 5
goest; how know we the way? Jesus saith unto him, I 6
am the way, and the truth, and the life: no one cometh
unto the Father, but by me.

7-15. Oneness with the Father.

If ye had known me, ye would have known my Father 7
also: from henceforth ye know him, and have seen him.
Philip saith unto him, Lord, shew us the Father, and it 8
sufficeth us. Jesus saith unto him, Have I been so long 9
time with you, and dost thou not know me, Philip? he
that hath seen me hath seen the Father; how sayest thou,
Shew us the Father? Believest thou not that I am in 10
the Father, and the Father in me? the words that I say
unto you I speak not from myself: but the Father abiding

---

6. I am the way. Christ is the way to truth—the means
of attaining truth in its highest sense; also the way to life and
salvation, which is life in its highest form. He is the 'new and
living way' by which we enter the holy place (Heb. x. 20).

the truth. Absolute truth is found in Christ alone. 'Truth
as it is in Jesus' (Eph. iv. 21) is perfect truth, i.e. not only
truth in word and act, but truth as perfection of nature, exact
conformity to an ideal, achievement of a purpose, harmonious
working of parts.

the life, the energy, or activity of the truth as manifested in
the life of Christ. Christ is essentially the Christian life; comp.
'I am the resurrection and the life' (ch. xi. 25); 'to me to live
is Christ' (Phil. i. 21).

9. dost thou not know me? In a sense the disciples were
very far from knowing Christ while He was still with them. It
was only after the Ascension and the coming of the Holy Ghost
that they knew Him in His Divine nature or in uncorruptness (ἐν
ἀφθαρσίᾳ), Ephes. vi. 24; comp. 2 Cor. v. 16, 'even though we
have known Jesus Christ after the flesh, yet now know we him
so no more.'

he that hath seen me hath seen the Father. This 'seeing of
Christ' implied a complete understanding of His Divine nature;
and as a consequence, discerning the correspondence between the
works of God as revealed in the O.T. and the works of Jesus.

10, 11. The **words** and the **works** of Jesus, as the *Logos* or
Interpreter of God, are the words and the works of the Father.

11 in me doeth his works. Believe me that I am in the
Father, and the Father in me : or else believe me for the
12 very works' sake. Verily, verily, I say unto you, He that
believeth on me, the works that I do shall he do also ;
and greater *works* than these shall he do ; because I go
13 unto the Father. And whatsoever ye shall ask in my
name, that will I do, that the Father may be glorified in
14 the Son. If ye shall ask me anything in my name, that
15 will I do. If ye love me, ye will keep my commandments.

16–31. The promise of the Comforter or Paraclete.

16 And I will pray the Father, and he shall give you another
17 Comforter, that he may be with you for ever, *even* the

---

12. greater works than these shall he do. The reference is
to works done by the inspiration and operation of the Holy
Ghost, whose coming was made possible by the departure of
Jesus. Among these works are the wonderful results of the
preaching of the Apostles, and especially of St Paul, and still
later the mission work of the Church and the conversion of
whole nations to the faith of Christ.

13. in my name, as an ambassador speaks in the name of his
king. The prayer of the disciple has the force of a prayer of
Christ Himself.

14. If ye shall ask me. The last word is restored to the text
in R.V. on high authority. As early instances of prayer addressed
immediately to Christ see Acts i. 24, vii. 59, 60.

15. The condition both of answer to prayer (*vv.* 13, 14) and
of the coming of the Spirit (*v.* 16) is keeping the commandments
of Jesus.

ye will keep my commandments, for 'keep my commandments,' A.V. Obedience is a consequence of love, and
perfect obedience to the will of Christ is union with Him.

16. another Comforter, or 'Advocate,' *marg.*, which is a
literal rendering of the Greek word παράκλητος (Paraclete), and
on the whole is preferable to 'Comforter'; comp. 1 John ii. 1, 'we
have an Advocate (or helper, *marg.*) with the Father, Jesus
Christ the righteous,' where the term is applied to Christ. From
the sense of 'Advocate,' one summoned to help, comes the
secondary meaning, a 'Comforter.' The allusion to 'the promise
of the Father,' Acts i. 4, proves that these words of Jesus were
known to St Luke and to the Church. See also Rom. viii. 9,
where the fulfilment of this promise is taken for granted : 'If any

Spirit of truth : whom the world cannot receive ; for it beholdeth him not, neither knoweth him : ye know him ; for he abideth with you, and shall be in you. I will not 18 leave you desolate : I come unto you. Yet a little while, 19 and the world beholdeth me no more ; but ye behold me : because I live, ye shall live also. In that day ye shall 20 know that I am in my Father, and ye in me, and I in you. He that hath my commandments, and keepeth them, he 21 it is that loveth me : and he that loveth me shall be loved of my Father, and I will love him, and will manifest myself unto him. Judas (not Iscariot) saith unto 22

---

man hath not the Spirit of Christ he is none of his.' Note that in this passage the Spirit of God and the Spirit of Christ are used as convertible terms.

17. the Spirit of truth. The Spirit who would lead the disciples of Christ into all truth ; and teach them 'as truth is in Jesus.'

ye know him. Jesus by His words and acts had enabled His disciples to recognise the works of the Spirit.

18. desolate, or 'orphans,' *marg.*, for 'comfortless,' A.V.

I come unto you. Comp. *infra v.* 21, 'I will manifest myself unto him.' This promise of coming or manifestation was fulfilled by the appearance of Christ during the forty days after the Resurrection, to the comfort of St Peter and for the conversion of James the Lord's brother, and the instruction of all His disciples, Acts i. 2–8. Afterwards by His presence at the choice of Matthias, Acts i. 24, at the martyrdom of St Stephen, in the vision of St Peter, by His appearance to St Paul and Ananias and to St John, and in the history of the Church to His servants by a felt and realised presence (see Acts vii. 55, ix. 5, 10, x. 14, xvi. 7, R.V., xviii. 9, 10 ; Rev. i. 13, and *passim*).

19. I live. Jesus Christ is still living and working with His Church. The Gospels narrate only what He '*began* to do and teach' (Acts i. 1) ; comp. also Rev. i. 18, 'I was dead, and behold, I am alive for evermore.'

because I live, ye shall live also. Comp. 'to me to live is Christ,' Phil. i. 21.

20. In that day. Perhaps with a special reference to the Day of Pentecost—but 'that day' signifies all occasions when the presence of Christ is realised.

22. Judas, called Lebbæus or Thaddeus, Matt. x. 4 ; Mark iii. 18. The two names imply a union of courage and gentleness.

him, Lord, what is come to pass that thou wilt manifest
23 thyself unto us, and not unto the world ? Jesus answered
and said unto him, If a man love me, he will keep my word:
and my Father will love him, and we will come unto him,
24 and make our abode with him. He that loveth me not
keepeth not my words: and the word which ye hear is not
mine, but the Father's who sent me.

25 These things have I spoken unto you, while *yet* abiding
26 with you. But the Comforter, *even* the Holy Spirit, whom
the Father will send in my name, he shall teach you all
things, and bring to your remembrance all that I said unto
27 you. Peace I leave with you ; my peace I give unto

The note 'not Iscariot' is added to make it clear that the traitor
had not returned. See ch. xiii. 30.

what is come to pass, &c. The form of the question implies
disappointment at a supposed change of plan.

unto us, and not unto the world. Judas with the rest of the
Apostles still thought of a visible kingdom of God founded on a
grand manifestation of the Christ. Soon after the Resurrection
the disciples asked, 'dost thou at this time restore the kingdom
to Israel?' Acts i. 6.

23. make our abode with him. So St Paul teaches that
believers are 'a temple of the living God,' 2 Cor. vi. 16.

24. the word which ye hear, &c. These words are added in
order to emphasise and certify the promise which precedes.

26. the Comforter, even the Holy Spirit. The term 'Comforter' or 'Advocate' or 'Counsellor' (Greek *Paraclete*), and His
identification with the Holy Spirit are a fresh revelation to the
Apostles.

bring to your remembrance all that I said. The words
of Jesus when recalled by the Holy Spirit had a force and significance often unperceived at first. The Gospel of St John is
a striking instance of this. Often too in Christian experience
a word or thought long latent acquires meaning through special
circumstances.

27. Peace I leave with you. The conventional salutation of
an Oriental here gains a profound significance. It is the peace
and calmness brought to the soul by perfect trust in God. The
word occurs here for the first time in this Gospel, and is rare in
the synoptics : it is a frequent post-Ascension word ; see ch. xx.
19, 21, 26, where our Lord gives peace 'not as the world giveth.'
With St Paul it is frequent, but it is not found in the First
Epistle of St John.

you : not as the world giveth, give I unto you. Let not
your heart be troubled, neither let it be fearful. Ye heard 28
how I said to you, I go away, and I come unto you. If
ye loved me, ye would have rejoiced, because I go unto
the Father : for the Father is greater than I. And now I 29
have told you before it come to pass, that, when it is
come to pass, ye may believe. I will no more speak 30
much with you, for the prince of the world cometh : and
he hath nothing in me ; but that the world may know 31
that I love the Father, and as the Father gave me commandment, even so I do. Arise, let us go hence.

15 1–27. The Parable of the Vine, and the teaching of it.
The Union of the Disciples with Christ and with one
another.

I am the true vine, and my Father is the husbandman. **15**

---

not as the world giveth. The world gives its greeting of
'peace' in a thoughtless, unmeaning fashion. My gift is a real
one.
28. ye would have rejoiced, because I go to the Father.
Partly, because as friends ye would have rejoiced to see One
whom ye love so highly exalted; partly, because that change will
enable Me to be spiritually present with you always.
the Father is greater than I. Christ not 'glorified' as yet,
though 'equal to the Father as touching His Godhead,' is
'inferior to the Father as touching His manhood' (Creed of
St Athanasius).
29. ye may believe. They will be assured that the sense of
the presence of Christ is real, and not imaginary.
30. the prince of the world cometh. The hour of darkness
is at hand. Satan indeed has 'nothing in Christ,' has no claim
or power over Christ. Only by submission to death He does the
Father's will.

XV. 1. The last words of ch. xiv. shew that Jesus and His disciples have left the room—the scene of the Last Supper. They
probably passed through the streets of Jerusalem, and sat on the
slopes of the Valley of Kidron, when Jesus spoke to them again.
the true vine. The parable may have been suggested by a vine
growing within sight. Moreover the vine was a symbol of Israel.
Jesus therefore represents Himself as the true vine. But the
leading thought is the closeness of the union between Christ and
His disciples. Their very life depends on this union : just as the
life of the branches depends on the vitality of the trunk or stem.
my Father is the husbandman. The husbandman is also the

2 Every branch in me that beareth not fruit, he taketh it away : and every *branch* that beareth fruit, he cleanseth
3 it, that it may bear more fruit. Already ye are clean because of the word which I have spoken unto you.
4 Abide in me, and I in you. As the branch cannot bear fruit of itself, except it abide in the vine ; so neither can
5 ye, except ye abide in me. I am the vine, ye are the branches : He that abideth in me, and I in him, the same beareth much fruit : for apart from me ye can do nothing.
6 If a man abide not in me, he is cast forth as a branch, and is withered ; and they gather them, and cast them
7 into the fire, and they are burned. If ye abide in me, and my words abide in you, ask whatsoever ye will, and it
8 shall be done unto you. Herein is my Father glorified, that ye bear much fruit ; and *so* shall ye be my disciples.

---

owner. The same thought is found in the words : 'ye are Christ's, and Christ is God's,' 1 Cor. iii. 23.

2. taketh it away...cleanseth it, for 'purgeth,' A.V. Two processes in vine culture are named : (1) excision of unfruitful branches. (2) Pruning of the fruitful branches. The first is interpreted of nominal Christians, who are separated from Christ as being unworthy ; the second are believers, whose characters are formed and purified by the discipline of Christ.

3. ye are clean, in reference to 'cleanseth,' *v.* 2. For the Eleven this discipline has already operated through the word of Christ : comp. James i. 18, 'He brought us forth by the word of truth, that we should be a kind of first fruits of his creatures.'

4. Abide in me, and I in you. The ground principle of the Christian life, expressed by the 'in Christ' of St Paul, Rom. viii. 1, 2, and very frequently ; less frequently by St Peter (1 Pet. iii. 16, v. 10, 14), but not elsewhere in N.T.

6. cast them into the fire, and they are burned. Comp. the parable of the tares, Matt. xiii. 40–42. It has been noted that possibly at this moment the operation of cutting off the unfruitful branches and burning them was going on in sight of Jesus and His disciples.

7. whatsoever ye will, for 'what ye will,' A.V. See ch. xiv. 13. The believer's will is conformed to the will of Christ. Therefore his prayers are answered.

8. Herein is my Father glorified, &c. As the husbandman takes pride in the fruitfulness of the vine, so is the Father glorified by the good works of His children.

shall ye be, better, 'shall ye become.'

Even as the Father hath loved me, I also have loved you: 9
abide ye in my love. If ye keep my commandments, ye 10
shall abide in my love ; even as I have kept my Father's
commandments, and abide in his love. These things 11
have I spoken unto you, that my joy may be in you, and
that your joy may be fulfilled. This is my commandment, 12
that ye love one another, even as I have loved you.
Greater love hath no man than this, that a man lay down 13
his life for his friends. Ye are my friends, if ye do the 14
things which I command you. No longer do I call you 15
servants ; for the servant knoweth not what his lord
doeth : but I have called you friends ; for all things that
I heard from my Father I have made known unto you.
Ye did not choose me, but I chose you, and appointed 16
you, that ye should go and bear fruit, and *that* your fruit

9, 10. The relation between Christ and His Apostles must
be precisely that between Christ and the Father—based upon
obedience and love.

11. The joy of Christ arose from the consciousness of the
Father's love. This joy He will impart to His disciples. This is
what Brother Lawrence describes as 'an habitual, silent and
secret conversation of the soul with God, which often causes me
joys and raptures inwardly, and sometimes also outwardly, so
great that I am forced to use means to moderate them, and
prevent their appearance to others.' *The Practice of the Presence
of God*, p. 25.

12. even as I have loved you. That is with a self-sacrificing
love; see Eph. v. 1, 2 'Walk in love, even as Christ also loved
you, and gave himself up for us, an offering and a sacrifice to God.'

13. Greater love hath no man than this, &c. These words
must have touched Peter to the quick. He had just professed in
the same words (xiii. 37) to do this for Jesus, and had been
warned of failure. It is the highest point of Christian love, and
the essence of the Atonement.

15. No longer do I call you servants, or 'slaves.' It is
the manumission of the servants of Christ. The faithful slave
becomes a friend.

16. I chose you at a definite time (Matt. x. 1–5), and made
you my elect with a special work to do ; comp. Acts i. 2 ; Matt.
xxviii. 19.

your fruit should abide. The results of the Apostles' labours
are with us to-day.

should abide: that whatsoever ye shall ask of the Father
17 in my name, he may give it you. These things I com-
18 mand you, that ye may love one another. If the world
hateth you, ye know that it hath hated me before *it hated*
19 *you.* If ye were of the world, the world would love its
own: but because ye are not of the world, but I chose
you out of the world, therefore the world hateth you.
20 Remember the word that I said unto you, A servant is
not greater than his lord. If they persecuted me, they
will also persecute you; if they kept my word, they will
21 keep yours also. But all these things will they do unto you
for my name's sake, because they know not him that sent
22 me. If I had not come and spoken unto them, they had
not had sin: but now they have no excuse for their sin.
23 He that hateth me hateth my Father also. If I had not
24 done among them the works which none other did, they
had not had sin; but now have they both seen and hated
25 both me and my Father. But *this cometh to pass*, that the
word may be fulfilled that is written in their law, They
26 hated me without a cause. But when the Comforter is

---

18. the world, all who reject the revelation of God in Christ.
The first reference is to the Jews, but it includes all forms of
society constituted on merely human rules. The social life of
the Roman Empire was essentially hostile to the Kingdom of
God.

20. Remember the word, &c. See ch. xiii. 16; Matt. x. 24.
they will also persecute you. For three centuries this was
terribly true of the Christian Church. The name 'Christian'
carried with it a sentence of death.

21. they know not him that sent me. The true character
of God was revealed in Christ—the Word. Before Christ no
Jew had a complete conception of God.

22. they have no excuse for their sin. Christ has a claim
for recognition. Failure to recognise Him is sin.

24. the works of Christ, which include His sayings and
His character, were testimony which it was wilful sin to
resist.

25. They hated me without a cause. See Pss. xxxv. 19,
lxix. 4. The groundless hate from which the Psalmist suffered
was exemplified tenfold in Christ.

come, whom I will send unto you from the Father, *even*
the Spirit of truth, which proceedeth from the Father, he
shall bear witness of me: and ye also bear witness, 27
because ye have been with me from the beginning.

16 1–33. **The Departure of Jesus and the consequences of it.**
    (a) Persecution, 1–5.

These things have I spoken unto you, that ye should **16**
not be made to stumble. They shall put you out of the 2
synagogues: yea, the hour cometh, that whosoever killeth
you shall think that he offereth service unto God. And 3
these things will they do, because they have not known
the Father, nor me. But these things have I spoken unto 4
you, that when their hour is come, ye may remember
them, how that I told you. And these things I said not
unto you from the beginning, because I was with you.
But now I go unto him that sent me; and none of you 5
asketh me, Whither goest thou?

---

26. he shall bear witness of me. This inner witness of the
Spirit lies at the root of Christian theology: 'No man can say
Jesus is Lord, but in the Holy Spirit,' 1 Cor. xii. 3.
27. ye also bear witness. To be witnesses, and specially
witnesses of the Resurrection, was definitely the office of the
Apostles, as constituted by Christ, Acts i. 8, 22, 'ye shall be my
witnesses.' And to have been with Christ from the beginning of
His ministry was a recognised qualification of an Apostle, Acts
i. 21.

XVI. 1. made to stumble, for 'offended,' A.V.; rather, be
troubled or disconcerted, because you find persecution where you
expected victory and success.
2. put you out of the synagogues. See ch. ix. 22, 34,
xii. 42.
whosoever killeth you...service unto God. A further degree
of persecution. A misinformed conscience has been a frequent
motive with the persecutor. It was so with St Paul. Bishop
Westcott quotes from the Midrash: 'Every one that sheds the
blood of the wicked is as he that offereth an offering.'
4. So far from being a hindrance to faith, persecution will
add to faith as confirming the words of Jesus.
5. none of you asketh me, Whither goest thou? The

(b) Victory over the world by the power of the Holy Ghost, 6–16.

6 But because I have spoken these things unto you, sorrow
7 hath filled your heart.   Nevertheless I tell you the truth;
It is expedient for you that I go away: for if I go not
away, the Comforter will not come unto you; but if I go,
8 I will send him unto you.   And he, when he is come, will
convict the world in respect of sin, and of righteousness,
9 and of judgement: of sin, because they believe not on me;

desire of Jesus is that His disciples should dwell on His own future and their future rather than on the thought of separation. Therefore He encourages them to ask.

7. Comforter. Advocate or Helper, R.V. *margin.* **I will send him unto you.** See xiv. 26, 'whom the Father will send in my name.'

8. will convict, for 'will reprove,' A.V.   To convict is to condemn by or after a clear presentiment of facts.   The most telling indictment against an accused person is a statement of the offence in unmistakable and undeniable terms.   Such a statement is an appeal to conscience.   It awakens conscience or else it hardens it.   In the first instance **the world** meant the unbelieving Jews, and their grievous sin was the rejection of Christ, *v.* 9.

The first striking example, then, of conviction in respect of sin was on the Day of Pentecost, when St Peter speaking under the influence of the Holy Spirit presented the facts of the Gospel so plainly that the Jews and proselytes who heard him were 'pricked in their heart,' Acts ii. 37.

No nation or generation of men, no civilisation of any type, has ever justified or approved the condemnation of Christ; of this sin at least the world has been convinced and convicted.

But as the Gospel spread, the meaning both of the world and of sin was widened.   'The world' meant, and means, society in general.   In the first instance pagan society, steeped through and through with awful and indescribable sin.   Religion even was often organised impurity; and vice brought no sense of shame.   This was the world which the Holy Spirit convicted of sin by means of the Apostles and Evangelists of Jesus Christ. And this process of conviction is still going on.   And sin is still seen to be summed up in the rejection of Jesus Christ.   The principles which made the Jews hate Christ and put Him to death are still the moving forces of evil.

in respect of sin, i.e. will set the truth about sin clearly before men.   See last note.

of righteousness, because I go to the Father, and ye 10
behold me no more; of judgement, because the prince of 11
this world hath been judged. I have yet many things to 12
say unto you, but ye cannot bear them now. Howbeit 13
when he, the Spirit of truth, is come, he shall guide you
into all the truth: for he shall not speak from himself;
but what things soever he shall hear, *these* shall he speak:
and he shall declare unto you the things that are to come.
He shall glorify me: for he shall take of mine, and shall 14

---

10. of righteousness. The Jewish conception of righteousness was derived from the Pharisees. In respect of that righteousness of the letter St Paul before his conversion was 'blameless.' In Christ a new type of righteousness was revealed through the Holy Spirit by the preaching of the Apostles. This righteousness of God forms the content of the Gospel, Rom. i. 16.

This revelation of righteousness was only possible by the mission of the Holy Ghost consequent on the departure of Jesus Christ from the sight of His disciples. Only when He had gone to the Father could the righteousness exhibited in His life and work be viewed in its perfected completion.

11. of judgement, because the prince of this world hath been judged. The prince of this world is Satan. In the awful, prevailing wickedness of the ancient world it was not difficult to believe that the powers of evil were paramount. The 'throne of Satan' (Rev. ii. 13), which literally 'framed mischief by statute' (Ps. xciv. 20), was established in the Roman Empire. But Christ had already judged 'the prince of this world' at the beginning of His Ministry (Matt. iv. 10). The purpose and plan of Christ prevailed over Satan in the Temptation. See also Luke x. 18, 'I beheld Satan when he fell as lightning from heaven.' Though the struggle of good and evil is still going on, all that is best, and in reality strongest, in the world is enlisted on the side of Christ. Gradually the truth in respect of the judgment of Satan is recognised.

12. many things to say. These are at least in part contained in the Epistles and the Apocalypse and exhibited in the Acts. Godet remarks that ch. xiv. 26 contains the formula of the inspiration of the Gospels; this verse contains that of the Epistles and Apocalypse.

Among other things which the disciples could not bear now was the unconditional admission of the Gentiles—the relation of the Gospel to the Law—the full teaching about the death of Christ.

15 declare *it* unto you. All things whatsoever the Father
hath are mine: therefore said I, that he taketh of mine,
16 and shall declare *it* unto you. A little while, and ye
behold me no more; and again a little while, and ye shall
see me.

(c) Sorrow turned into joy, 17-24.

17 *Some* of his disciples therefore said one to another, What
is this that he saith unto us, A little while, and ye behold
me not; and again a little while, and ye shall see me : and,
18 Because I go to the Father? They said therefore, What
is this that he saith, A little while? We know not what
19 he saith. Jesus perceived that they were desirous to ask
him, and he said unto them, Do ye inquire among yourselves concerning this, that I said, A little while, and ye
behold me not, and again a little while, and ye shall see
20 me? Verily, verily, I say unto you, that ye shall weep

---

15. All things whatsoever the Father hath are mine. Nowhere has Jesus declared more impressively or more completely
stated His equality with the Father, or the Divine character of
His gifts to His Church.

16. a little while, and ye shall see me. The reference must
be in the first instance to Pentecost. The return of Christ was
through the Holy Spirit and made possible by His going to the
Father. St Paul testifies to the reality of this return, to himself,
and to believers generally : 'Seeing that ye seek a proof of
Christ that speaketh in me…Know ye not as to your own selves,
that Jesus Christ is in you? unless indeed ye be reprobate,'
2 Cor. xiii. 3, 5.

Note the distinction brought out by the R.V. between 'behold'
in the first part of the verse and 'see' in the second part. 'To
behold' relates to things external, see Matt. xxvii. 55, 'to see'
relates to things spiritual and is connected with the word
rendered 'vision' ($\check{o}\psi\iota s$). The distinction is kept up in the
following verse.

The words 'because I go to the Father,' A.V., are here rightly
omitted in R.V.

19. Note here the readiness of Jesus to answer questions, and
the awe which prevented the disciples asking. Comp. Lk. ix. 45,
'they were afraid to ask him.'

20. Jesus here foretells precisely the effect of the Crucifixion
followed by the Resurrection—sorrow turned into joy.

and lament, but the world shall rejoice: ye shall be sorrowful, but your sorrow shall be turned into joy. A 21 woman when she is in travail hath sorrow, because her hour is come: but when she is delivered of the child, she remembereth no more the anguish, for the joy that a man is born into the world. And ye therefore now have sorrow: 22 but I will see you again, and your heart shall rejoice, and your joy no one taketh away from you. And in that day 23 ye shall ask me nothing. Verily, verily, I say unto you, If ye shall ask anything of the Father, he will give it you in my name. Hitherto have ye asked nothing in my name: 24 ask, and ye shall receive, that your joy may be fulfilled.

(d) 25-33.   The relations of the Disciples to the Father.

These things have I spoken unto you in proverbs: the 25 hour cometh, when I shall no more speak unto you in proverbs, but shall tell you plainly of the Father. In that 26 day ye shall ask in my name: and I say not unto you, that I will pray the Father for you; for the Father himself 27 loveth you, because ye have loved me, and have believed that I came forth from the Father. I came out from the 28

---

22. your joy no one taketh away from you, because 'Christ being raised from the dead dieth no more,' Rom. vi. 9. There can be no separation from the love of Christ glorified and 'in uncorruptness,' Eph. vi. 24.

23. ye shall ask me nothing, i.e. ask me no question; because in the Holy Spirit both their knowledge and their power shall be complete.

If ye shall ask, i.e. make request—a different word from 'ask' above *v.* 23 (*a*).

25. These things have I spoken unto you in proverbs, or parables, A.V. and R.V. *marg.* Not only had Jesus used illustrations such as the vine, or childbearing, but many of His more direct sayings were mystical, and would not be understood until after the Ascension—when the fuller revelation would come, which would make all things plain.

27. the Father himself loveth you, the access to the Father would be immediate, because the Son is One with the Father.

28. I came out from the Father, &c. This verse expresses the four great truths: (1) of the humiliation of Christ; He

Father, and am come into the world: again, I leave the
29 world, and go unto the Father. His disciples say, Lo,
now speakest thou plainly, and speakest no proverb.
30 Now know we that thou knowest all things, and needest
not that any man should ask thee: by this we believe that
31 thou camest forth from God. Jesus answered them, Do
32 ye now believe? Behold, the hour cometh, yea, is come,
that ye shall be scattered, every man to his own, and shall
leave me alone: and *yet* I am not alone, because the
33 Father is with me. These things have I spoken unto you,
that in me ye may have peace. In the world ye have
tribulation: but be of good cheer; I have overcome the
world.

> 17. The intercessory Prayer of Christ—the great High Priest—for
> Himself, 1–5; for His Disciples, 6–19; for His Church,
> 20–26.

17   These things spake Jesus; and lifting up his eyes to

'emptied himself' (Phil. ii. 7); (2) the Incarnation; (3) the
sacrificial Death; (4) the Ascension.
   29. Lo, now speakest thou plainly. This great revelation
casts a flood of light on the minds of the Apostles. All seems
clear and proved.
   31. Do ye now believe? or perhaps better, Now ye do
believe. Comp. ch. xvii. 8, 'they believed that thou didst send
me.' Jesus does not cast a doubt on their belief at the moment;
only He warns them that temporarily at least it will be shattered.
   32. to his own, i.e. to his own home. See ch. xix. 27.
   33. that in me ye may have peace. Even the temporary
defection would not remove the peace, nor could the persecution
which awaited them in the world. They would return to the
Master whom they had recognised as One with the Father
(*v.* 32), and in their tribulation they would remember that the
victory was with Christ. Comp. 1 Cor. xv. 57, 'Thanks be to
God, which giveth us the victory through our Lord Jesus Christ.'
   XVII. This last sublime utterance of the Saviour, 'in words
most simple, in sense most profound' (Bengel), seems to lie above
the reach of comment. It is at once a prayer, an instruction, a
prophecy, a last will or testament, and a consecration of Priest as
well as Victim. Jesus manifests Himself as an Advocate or
Paraclete with the Father for His disciples.
   1. lifting up his eyes to heaven, the description of an eye-
witness.

heaven, he said, Father, the hour is come; glorify thy
Son, that the Son may glorify thee: even as thou 2
gavest him authority over all flesh, that whatsoever
thou hast given him, to them he should give eternal life.
And this is life eternal, that they should know thee the 3
only true God, and him whom thou didst send, *even* Jesus
Christ. I glorified thee on the earth, having accomplished 4
the work which thou hast given me to do. And now, O 5
Father, glorify thou me with thine own self with the glory
which I had with thee before the world was. I manifested 6
thy name unto the men whom thou gavest me out of the
world: thine they were, and thou gavest them to me; and
they have kept thy word. Now they know that all things 7

---

the hour is come, the hour appointed by the Father. See
ch. vii. 30, and comp. Gal. iv. 4.

glorify thy Son. To glorify is to manifest, see *vv.* 4 and 6.
The Son was further glorified, by (1) His death on the Cross:
'Wherefore (because He was obedient unto death) God highly
exalted him, and gave unto him the name, which is above every
name' (Phil. ii. 9); by (2) the Resurrection (Rom. i. 4); and
(3) by the spread of the Gospel in the world.

3. this is life eternal, &c. Perfect knowledge of God is
likeness to God. 'We shall be like him, for we shall see him even
as he is,' 1 John iii. 2. So that knowledge of God and Christ-
likeness and eternal life are one and the same thing. Comp.
'Whom truly to know is everlasting life' (Prayer-Book). Here
only does our Lord apply the term 'Christ' to Himself, though
on other occasions He accepts the title. See ch. iv. 26 and
Matt. xvi. 17; Mk xiv. 61, 62.

4. having accomplished the work, &c. The same thought
as in the word from the Cross, 'It is finished.' Ch. xix. 30.

5. glorify thou me with thine own self, &c. For this glory
of Christ 'before the world was made,' see Phil. iii. 6, and
Col. i. 15-19.

6. manifested thy name. The life and work and death of
Jesus were a manifestation of God as Father, whose love was
shewn above all in the mission and death of Christ.

7, 8. they know, &c. The Apostles are able to discern the
teaching and works of God the Father in those of Jesus: comp.
1 Cor. xii. 3, and 1 John iv. 14, 'We have beheld and bear
witness that the Father hath sent the Son to be the Saviour of
the world.'

8 whatsoever thou hast given me are from thee: for the words which thou gavest me I have given unto them; and they received *them*, and knew of a truth that I came forth 9 from thee, and they believed that thou didst send me. I pray for them: I pray not for the world, but for those 10 whom thou hast given me; for they are thine: and all things that are mine are thine, and thine are mine: and 11 I am glorified in them. And I am no more in the world, and these are in the world, and I come to thee. Holy Father, keep them in thy name which thou hast given me, 12 that they may be one, even as we *are*. While I was with them, I kept them in thy name which thou hast given me: and I guarded them, and not one of them perished, but the son of perdition; that the scripture might be 13 fulfilled. But now I come to thee; and these things I speak in the world, that they may have my joy fulfilled in 14 themselves. I have given them thy word; and the world

---

9. I pray for them. In a spiritual way and with a special word (ἐρωτῶ) Jesus prays for His Elect—for those who respond to His teaching, and who recognise in Him the Christ. This is of course consistent with the truth that Christ died for all men. But 'the world' was not prepared to receive the gifts which Jesus asks for His disciples.

10. I am glorified in them. The Apostles will be the instruments of spreading the knowledge of Christ in the world, and it is they who will represent to the world the character of Christ.

11. keep them in thy name, i.e. in their faith and holiness and separation from the world, through which God is made known to the world. For 'name,' see below *vv.* 12, 26.

which thou hast given me. See Phil. ii. 9 cited above *v.* 3. There 'the name above every name' is the name of God.

that they may be one. See Rom. xii. 5; Eph. i. 10, ii. 21, 22, and iv. 4, where the unity of the Christian Church is illustrated by the unity of a temple, each several building of which is fitly framed together.

12. kept them in thy name, i.e. in the revelation of God, in His holiness. It is a beautiful expression of Christ's continual watchfulness over the lives of His disciples.

13. my joy, the joy of returning to the Father. This joy He wished His disciples to share.

hated them, because they are not of the world, even as I
am not of the world.   I pray not that thou shouldest take 15
them from the world, but that thou shouldest keep them
from the evil *one*.   They are not of the world, even as I 16
am not of the world.   Sanctify them in the truth: thy 17
word is truth.   As thou didst send me into the world, 18
even so sent I them into the world.   And for their sakes 19
I sanctify myself, that they themselves also may be
sanctified in truth.   Neither for these only do I pray, but 20
for them also that believe on me through their word; that 21
they may all be one; even as thou, Father, *art* in me,
and I in thee, that they also may be in us: that the world
may believe that thou didst send me.   And the glory 22
which thou hast given me I have given unto them; that

---

15.   The prayer of Jesus is that the disciples should still be in
the world but not of the world.   See Rom. xii. 2.

from the evil one, for 'from the evil,' A.V.   The same
change is made from the A.V. of the Lord's Prayer.

17.   Sanctify them in the truth: thy word is truth. Comp.
'Of his own will he brought us forth by the word of truth that
we should be a kind of firstfruits of his creatures,' James i. 18.
Comp. the words of the *Te Deum*: 'Make them to be numbered
with thy saints in glory everlasting.'

18.   As thou didst send me, &c.   Comp. ch. x. 36, 'Say ye
of him, whom the Father sanctified and sent into the world?'
&c.   Jesus Christ then was sanctified or consecrated for His
mission.   He was set apart for the special work of redemption.
But the redemption was by means of sacrifice.   Therefore He
was sanctified or consecrated both to be a sacrifice for sin, and
also to be the High Priest to offer the sacrifice, and to intercede.
'He ever liveth to make intercession,' Heb. vii. 25.

20.   for them also that believe on me through their word.
A thought reaching through all time to all disciples of Christ in
every age.

21.   that they may all be one.   The unity of believers would
be a magnificent proof to the world of the truth of Christianity.
This proof is withheld through sin.   But the prayer for unity is
one which should be offered unceasingly in the Church.

22.   the glory which thou hast given me, this glory is
manifold—the glory of the Father's love, which Christ imparts
to them.   Again, the glory of the mission of the Son, and the

23 they may be one, even as we *are* one; I in them, and
   thou in me, that they may be perfected into one; that
   the world may know that thou didst send me, and lovedst
24 them, even as thou lovedst me. Father, that which thou
   hast given me, I will that, where I am, they also may be
   with me; that they may behold my glory, which thou hast
   given me: for thou lovedst me before the foundation of the
25 world. O righteous Father, the world knew thee not, but
   I knew thee; and these knew that thou didst send me;
26 and I made known unto them thy name, and will make it
   known; that the love wherewith thou lovedst me may be
   in them, and I in them.

18 1–11. The Passage of the Kidron and the Arrest of Jesus,
   Matt. xxvi. 47–56; Mk xv. 43–50; Lk. xxii. 47–53.

18   When Jesus had spoken these words, he went forth with
   his disciples over the brook Kidron, where was a garden,

---

glory of the manifestation of Christ and of God in Christ. The
glory therefore imparted to the disciples is that they are one with
the Father and the Son in work and mission, and in partaking
of the Divine nature. See Ephes. i. 6–12.

23. perfected into one, for 'made perfect in one,' A.V.
The correction of the R.V. gives the sense of *growth* into
perfection, an essential note of the indwelling Christ. See
Eph. ii. 21, iv. 15.

24. may be with me. See 2 Tim. ii. 11.

that they may behold my glory. See 2 Cor. iii. 18.

25. righteous. Here only in this Gospel is the term
'righteous' ascribed to God. On this 'equitableness' of God
Jesus bases His confidence in asking for special blessings for
His disciples.

the world knew thee not, this very book is full of proofs of
this. The power of recognising God in Christ is a condition of
discipleship.

26. thy name. The name of God is that by which He
Himself, His character and attributes, are known, as e.g. His
love and righteousness, both indicated in these verses.

XVIII. 1. went forth, from Jerusalem, perhaps from the
Temple.

the brook Kidron, the dark stream, like our 'Blackwater,'
named several times in the O.T., as 2 Sam. xv. 23; 1 Kings ii. 37,

XVIII gap

into the which he entered, himself and his disciples. Now 2
Judas also, which betrayed him, knew the place : for Jesus
oft-times resorted thither with his disciples. Judas then, 3
having received the band *of soldiers*, and officers from
the chief priests and the Pharisees, cometh thither with
lanterns and torches and weapons. Jesus therefore, 4
knowing all the things that were coming upon him, went
forth, and saith unto them, Whom seek ye? They 5
answered him, Jesus of Nazareth. Jesus saith unto them,
I am *he*. And Judas also, which betrayed him, was
standing with them. When therefore he said unto them, 6
I am *he*, they went backward, and fell to the ground.
Again therefore he asked them, Whom seek ye? And 7
they said, Jesus of Nazareth. Jesus answered, I told you 8

---

here only in the N.T. At the present day the Kidron is a dry
torrent-bed filled only by winter rains. Dr Barclay however
discovered an underground channel with flowing water.

a garden, so named by St John only (Gethsemane = oil-press).
In the synoptic Gospels it is called a place or enclosure (χωρίον),
or small farm. The traditional site is about 50 yards from the
Kidron. The 'agony' in the Garden of Gethsemane is not
narrated by St John.

2. which betrayed him, literally ' who was betraying him.'

oft-times resorted. Bishop Westcott suggests that the owner
of Gethsemane was a disciple of Jesus.

3. the band of soldiers, for ' a band,' A.V., *marg.* cohort—
more probably *the maniple*, a body of 200 men, stationed in
Antonia, the Roman castle overlooking the Temple courts.

4. knowing all the things that were coming upon him, a
note which marks the unshrinking courage of Jesus. His hour
had come and He is obedient to His Father's will. St John
does not mention the kiss of Judas. The synoptics omit the
effect of the words of Jesus on those who were sent to take Him
(*v.* 6). Comp. ch. vii. 45.

5. was standing with them, for, 'stood with them,' A.V., one
of the instances where the tense makes the picture vivid. John
saw the betrayer standing with the enemies of Jesus, comp. ch.
i. 35 and *vv.* 18 and 25 *infra*, where the same change is made
with the same effect.

7. therefore, because they were hesitating to execute their
purpose.

C.   **8**

that I am *he*: if therefore ye seek me, let these go their
9 way: that the word might be fulfilled which he spake,
Of those whom thou hast given me I lost not one.
10 Simon Peter therefore having a sword drew it, and struck
the high priest's servant, and cut off his right ear. Now
11 the servant's name was Malchus. Jesus therefore said
unto Peter, Put up the sword into the sheath: the cup
which the Father hath given me, shall I not drink it?

12-14 and 19-23. Jesus is led to Annas.

12 So the band and the chief captain, and the officers of the
13 Jews, seized Jesus and bound him, and led him to Annas

---

8. let these go their way. Jesus, as the Paraclete, intercedes
for His own disciples; as afterwards He interceded for the
soldiers, who were nailing Him to the cross.

9. See ch. xvii. **12.**

10. struck the high priest's servant, &c. In doing so St
Peter was acting up to his word given, ch. xiii. **37.** The act
might well have involved dying with his Master. There is no
lack of the soldier's physical courage in St Peter; where he fails
is in moral courage.

Malchus. St John alone gives the name of this servant and
of St Peter: both he and St Luke note that it was the right ear.
There were reasons for reticence when the earlier Gospels were
preached or written.

11. the cup which the Father hath given, &c. See Matt.
xxvi. **42**; Mk xiv. **36**: the reference is to the immediately
preceding incident of 'the agony,' comp. also Matt. xx. **22** and
Isaiah li. **22.**

12-14. This preliminary proceeding and informal questioning
(*vv.* 19-24) is not named by the synoptists, who record (1) an
informal trial before Caiaphas and some members of the Sanhedrin, at night, Matt. xxvi. **57-68**; Mk xiv. **53-75**; Luke xxii.
54, 63-65, (2) a formal trial before the Sanhedrin, Caiaphas
presiding, related by Luke xxii. **66-71** and mentioned by Matt.
xxvii. **1** and Mark xv. **1.**

12. the band. See above, *v.* **3.**

the chief captain or military tribune, *marg.* See Acts iv. **1**;
1 Chron. ix. **11.** It must be remembered that the Temple was
a fortress as well as a sanctuary and place of worship. The
captain of the Temple was in command of the Levitical guard.
He ranked next in dignity to the high priest.

seized Jesus and bound him. The aggressive act of St Peter
dispelled the first hesitation of the soldiers.

first; for he was father in law to Caiaphas, which was high
priest that year. Now Caiaphas was he which gave 14
counsel to the Jews, that it was expedient that one man
should die for the people.

15–18. The first denial of St Peter. Matt. xxvi. 58, 69, 70;
    Mk xiv. 54, 66; Lk. xxii. 54–57.

And Simon Peter followed Jesus, and *so did* another 15
disciple. Now that disciple was known unto the high
priest, and entered in with Jesus into the court of the high
priest; but Peter was standing at the door without. So 16
the other disciple, which was known unto the high priest,
went out and spake unto her that kept the door, and
brought in Peter. The maid therefore that kept the door 17
saith unto Peter, Art thou also *one* of this man's disciples?
He saith, I am not. Now the servants and the officers 18
were standing *there*, having made a fire of coals; for it
was cold; and they were warming themselves: and Peter
also was with them, standing and warming himself.

19–23. Questioning by the high priest.

The high priest therefore asked Jesus of his disciples, 19
and of his teaching. Jesus answered him, I have spoken 20
openly to the world; I ever taught in synagogues, and in

---

14. See ch. xi. 50.
15. **another disciple**, almost without doubt St John, whose
home was in Jerusalem.
    entered in with Jesus, an act of great courage.
17. **therefore**, for 'then' A.V.; the maid saw that St Peter
was a friend of St John.
    Art thou also, i.e. as well as John, whom she knew to be
a disciple, and who did not conceal the fact.
18. **were standing there…were warming themselves**, &c.
These imperfects give a much more vivid picture than the definite
tenses of the A.V. *stood…warmed*.
19. **The high priest**. According to most editors Caiaphas;
but Annas is also called high priest, Acts iv. 6, and if Caiaphas
is meant a difficulty arises in regard to *v.* 24. The passage is
probably to be referred to the informal hearing before Annas.

the temple, where all the Jews come together; and in
21 secret spake I nothing. Why askest thou me? ask them
that have heard *me*, what I spake unto them: behold,
22 these know the things which I said. And when he had
said this, one of the officers standing by struck Jesus with
his hand, saying, Answerest thou the high priest so?
23 Jesus answered him, If I have spoken evil, bear witness
of the evil: but if well, why smitest thou me?

> **24-27.** Informal trial before Caiaphas. The second and third
> denials of St Peter. These denials probably took place at
> the first *informal* trial before Caiaphas, narrated Matt. xxvi.
> 57-75; Mk xiv. 53-72; Lk. xxii. 54 and 63-65. The
> trial before the Council or Sanhedrin is noted Matthew
> xxvii. 1, Mark xv. 1; and given at length Luke xxii.
> 66-71.

24 Annas therefore sent him bound unto Caiaphas the
high priest.
25   Now Simon Peter was standing and warming himself.
They said therefore unto him, Art thou also *one* of his
26 disciples? He denied, and said, I am not. One of the
servants of the high priest, being a kinsman of him whose
ear Peter cut off, saith, Did not I see thee in the garden
27 with him? Peter therefore denied again: and straightway
the cock crew.

----

21. Why askest thou me? To interrogate the prisoner
directly was an irregular proceeding; the examination should be
by witnesses.
22. with his hand, &c., or, with a rod, *marg.*
25. was standing and warming himself. Again note the
descriptiveness of the imperfect tenses as compared with 'stood
and warmed himself' A.V. It was the light of the fire which
enabled the bystanders to recognise St Peter. This is indicated
by 'therefore.' 'They said therefore unto him.' See Luke
xxii. 56.
26. a kinsman of him, &c. A note of St John's personal
knowledge, and acquaintance with the household of the high
priest.

28—19 15. The delivery to Pontius Pilate. The Roman trial.
The trial before Pontius Pilate consisted of two parts: (a) a
preliminary examination (for which there is a technical legal
phrase, Lk. xxiii. 14): (b) a final trial and sentence to death.
The *remission* to Herod, recorded by St Luke only, xxiii.
7–11, took place between the two Roman trials (a) and (b).
Matt. xxvii. 11–31; Mk xv. 2–20; Lk. xxiii. 2–25.

They lead Jesus therefore from Caiaphas into the palace : 28
and it was early; and they themselves entered not into
the palace, that they might not be defiled, but might eat
the passover. Pilate therefore went out unto them, and 29
saith, What accusation bring ye against this man? They 30
answered and said unto him, If this man were not an

---

28. from Caiaphas, rather, from the house of Caiaphas
(Dr Field).

the palace, or *Prætorium, marg.* The Roman tribunal, or
judgment hall.

that they might not be defiled, by entering a house from
which leaven might not have been removed.

but might eat the passover. These words prove conclusively
that the Last Supper was not the regular paschal meal.

29. Pontius **Pilate,** a Roman of equestrian rank, was the
governor, or more accurately the Procurator of Judæa, which
after the banishment of Archelaus (see Matt. ii. 22) had been
placed under the direct government of Rome, and attached as a
dependency to Syria. Pilate filled this office during the last ten
years of the reign of Tiberius (A.D. 26–36), to whom he was
directly responsible as Procurator Cæsaris. His rule was most
unsympathetic, and stained by many acts of cruelty, see Lk. xiii.
1. He is said to have made an official report to Tiberius of our
Lord's trial and condemnation. Nothing is known for certain of
his subsequent history, except that he was summoned to Rome
for maladministration. The traditions connecting him with
Vienne in Gaul, or with Mt Pilatus in Switzerland, are un-
trustworthy.

What accusation bring ye, &c.? It was competent, and
would have been the usual course, for Pilate to accept the
verdict of the Sanhedrin and carry it out; which indeed he
eventually did. The trial before him, so far as it was a trial,
ended in a verdict of 'Not guilty.'

30. St John does not name the charges brought against Jesus
by the Sanhedrin. They are given by St Luke as (1) perverting
the nation; (2) forbidding to give tribute to Cæsar; (3) saying he
himself is Christ a King (Luke xxiii. 2).

evil-doer, we should not have delivered him up unto thee.
31 Pilate therefore said unto them, Take him yourselves, and
judge him according to your law. The Jews said unto
32 him, It is not lawful for us to put any man to death: that
the word of Jesus might be fulfilled, which he spake,
signifying by what manner of death he should die.

33   Pilate therefore entered again into the palace, and
called Jesus, and said unto him, Art thou the King of the
34 Jews? Jesus answered, Sayest thou this of thyself, or did
35 others tell it thee concerning me? Pilate answered, Am
I a Jew? Thine own nation and the chief priests delivered
36 thee unto me: what hast thou done? Jesus answered, My
kingdom is not of this world: if my kingdom were of this
world, then would my servants fight, that I should not be

---

32. that the word of Jesus might be fulfilled. See ch. iii.
14, viii. 28, xii. 32, and comp. Matt. xx. 19 and xxvi. 2.

33. Art thou the King of the Jews? In reference to the
accusation made by the Sanhedrin; see Lk. xxiii. 2. The
title 'King of the Jews' however is not an O.T. expression, and
is used by Gentiles only in the N.T. as here and Matt. ii. 2, and
by the soldiers in the Prætorium (Matt. xxvii. 29) and at the
Cross (Luke xxiii. 37). The priests and scribes use the term
'King of Israel.'

36. My kingdom is not of this world. Jesus does not deny
His Kingship, indeed He claims a kingdom; 'My Kingdom,' He
says, 'is not of this world.' Thus He refutes the charge of
treason which the Jews wished to convey to Pilate, but claims a
different and a much wider sovereignty than a kingdom of the
Jews.

not of this world. The aims and standard of dignity and
right in Christ's kingdom are moral and religious and spiritual,
not based on force or wealth or rank. The kingdom of God is
righteousness and peace and joy in the Holy Ghost (Rom. xiv.
17); not luxury ('eating and drinking'), see Matt. vi. 33,
xx. 26, and comp. Acts i. 8, where in answer to the question,
'Wilt thou at this time restore the Kingdom to Israel?' our Lord
answers, 'ye shall receive power when the Holy Ghost is come
upon you': shewing that the source of power in the kingdom of
God is spiritual, not earthly or temporal.

then would my servants fight. The Jews, not the Romans,
are contemplated as Christ's earthly enemies.

delivered to the Jews: but now is my kingdom not from
hence.   Pilate therefore said unto him, Art thou a king 37
then? Jesus answered, Thou sayest that I am a king.   To
this end have I been born, and to this end am I come
into the world, that I should bear witness unto the truth.
Every one that is of the truth heareth my voice.   Pilate 38
saith unto him, What is truth?

And when he had said this, he went out again unto the
Jews, and saith unto them, I find no crime in him.   But 39
ye have a custom, that I should release unto you one at
the passover: will ye therefore that I release unto you the
King of the Jews?   They cried out therefore again, saying, 40
Not this man, but Barabbas. Now Barabbas was a robber.

Then Pilate therefore took Jesus, and scourged him. 19

---

37. Thou sayest that I am a king. A form of assent.
Christ acknowledges His Kingship, the essence of which is
witnessing to the truth.   His subjects are all who respond to
this witnessing.

38. What is truth? Observe how from a tone of scornfulness
and irony Pilate descends to the position of a learner or disciple
of Jesus.   It is a note of the wonderful personal ascendency and
of the impression which He made even on men who were alien
or hostile to Him ; comp. above, *v.* 6.

no crime, nothing of which the law could take account, better
than 'fault,' A.V.

39. ye have a custom, &c.   The origin of the custom is quite
unknown; St Mark says, 'as he was wont to do unto them,' as
if the custom originated with Pilate.   The words, Lk. xxiii. 17,
A.V. 'of necessity he must release' are rejected in R.V.

40. Barabbas was a robber. St Mark and St Luke add that
he had 'committed murder in the insurrection,' Mark xv. 7;
Luke xxiii. 19; St Peter (Acts iii. 14, 15) brings out the full
meaning of this choice.   St John more clearly perhaps than the
synoptists shews the complete responsibility of the Jewish people
for the death of Christ.

XIX. 1. scourged him. Scourging usually preceded execution.
As inflicted by the Roman soldiers it was a cruel torture, often
fatal.   In this case Pilate hoped that this punishment would
satisfy the Jews : 'I will therefore chastise him and release him'
(Luke xxiii. 16).

2 And the soldiers plaited a crown of thorns, and put it on his
3 head, and arrayed him in a purple garment; and they
came unto him, and said, Hail, King of the Jews! and
4 they struck him with their hands. And Pilate went out
again, and saith unto them, Behold, I bring him out to
5 you, that ye may know that I find no crime in him. Jesus
therefore came out, wearing the crown of thorns and the
purple garment. And *Pilate* saith unto them, Behold, the
6 man! When therefore the chief priests and the officers
saw him, they cried out, saying, Crucify *him*, crucify *him*.
Pilate saith unto them, Take him yourselves, and crucify
7 him: for I find no crime in him. The Jews answered him,
We have a law, and by that law he ought to die, because

---

2. a crown of thorns. Fuel in Palestine consists in great
measure of thorny shrubs. It was probably from these as ready
to hand that the soldiers made the crown.

a purple garment, a scarlet robe or *chlamys* (Matt.). Clothed
in purple (Mark). It was either a worn-out plaid (*chlamys*)
belonging to Pilate, or a general's cloak (*paludamentum*).
'Purple' is used of any bright colour, so that 'scarlet' and
'purple' may have the same meaning.

3. they came unto him. These words are omitted in A.V.
The tense gives the picture of the soldiers marching past, one by
one, in mockery.

4. Pilate went out again, &c. St John narrates the struggle
in Pilate's mind, and his effort to release Jesus, at greater length
than the synoptists: (1) He finds no crime in Him, *vv.* 4, 6.
(2) He was afraid, because Jesus 'made himself the Son of God,'
vv. 7, 8. (3) He even 'sought to release him,' *v.* 12. But
his fear of the Jews and of Cæsar overcame this weak and
cowardly magistrate.

5. Behold, the man! an appeal partly to compassion, partly
to pride : 'Can this miserable and humiliated prisoner be worthy
of your vindictiveness? Is he not rather an object of scorn?'

Many great painters have attempted to portray this scene; see
for instance the 'Ecce Homo' of Correggio in the National
Gallery, where 'the features of Christ express pain without
being in the least disfigured by it' (Waagen).

6. Take him yourselves, an attempt to evade responsibility.
Pilate does not say this officially as judge, and so the chief
priests understand him ; for they press the charge against Him.

7. We have a law, &c. See Levit. xxiv. 16.

he made himself the Son of God. When Pilate therefore 8
heard this saying, he was the more afraid: and he entered 9
into the palace again, and saith unto Jesus, Whence art
thou? But Jesus gave him no answer. Pilate therefore 10
saith unto him, Speakest thou not unto me? knowest thou
not that I have power to release thee, and have power
to crucify thee? Jesus answered him, Thou wouldest 11
have no power against me, except it were given thee from
above: therefore he that delivered me unto thee hath
greater sin. Upon this Pilate sought to release him: but 12
the Jews cried out, saying, If thou release this man, thou
art not Cæsar's friend: every one that maketh himself
a king speaketh against Cæsar. When Pilate therefore 13
heard these words, he brought Jesus out, and sat down on
the judgement-seat at a place called The Pavement, but

he made himself the Son of God. This accusation adds
to Pilate's terror (*v.* 8) and to his desire to release Jesus.
It was a fresh charge on the part of the Jews. On the other
charges Jesus had been acquitted.

9. gave him no answer. Jesus was silent because Pilate
knew that He was innocent. His origin had no bearing on the
justice or injustice of the death sentence.

11. given thee from above. This teaching of the Divine
source of all power however used, righteously or unrighteously,
should be noted. Comp. Rom. xiii. 1, and see Archbishop
Benson's *The Apocalypse,* p. 148 foll., on the increasing use of
the verb 'to give,' as 'the origin of all power is traced to
a higher Personal source.'

therefore...greater sin. Either, greater sin than Pilate; because Caiaphas sinned against greater knowledge, or possibility
of knowledge, than Pilate, who was but carrying out the sentence
of the Sanhedrin in accordance with Divine purpose (Acts ii. 23);
or, greater sin; because the most heinous kind of sin is to do
injustice by the forms of justice. Of this sin Caiaphas and the
Sanhedrin had been guilty.

12. If thou release this man, &c. This was the charge of
treason, the most serious charge which could be brought against
a Roman official. The vision of the implacable Tiberius in the
background clinched the argument for Pilate.   **speaketh
against,** better 'opposeth' as *marg.*

13. the judgement-seat, or tribunal, generally a raised plat-
form in the *basilica* or court; here a portable seat or throne

14 in Hebrew, Gabbatha. Now it was the Preparation of the
passover: it was about the sixth hour. And he saith
15 unto the Jews, Behold, your King! They therefore cried
out, Away with *him*, away with *him*, crucify him. Pilate
saith unto them, Shall I crucify your King? The chief
16 priests answered, We have no king but Cæsar. Then
therefore he delivered him unto them to be crucified.

---

placed upon **the Pavement**, a raised floor ornamented with
tessellated or mosaic work.

This 'pavement' may have been on the top of the stairs leading
from the tower Antonia to the Temple courts.   **Gabbatha** is
lit. the ridge of the house, i.e. of the Temple. See Westcott,
ad loc.

14.   the Preparation of the passover, i.e. the day before the
passover, the 14th Nisan, on which day the paschal lambs were
sacrificed with a view to the paschal meal in the evening. See
ch. xiii. 1, 29, and xviii. 28.

about the sixth hour. St Mark (xv. 25) says: 'It was the
third hour, and they crucified him'; and all the synoptists give
the sixth hour as the time when darkness fell on the scene. According to the usual reckoning these hours were respectively nine
o'clock in the morning and noon. St John however here places
the final sentence of Pilate at the sixth hour. One explanation
which has been offered of the discrepancy is that St John
reckoned the hours from midnight, and not, like the synoptists,
from sunrise. It seems however to be uncertain whether this
mode of reckoning was in use. Professor Ramsay notes that
although the Roman civil day was reckoned from midnight it
was not divided into hours. (*Expositor*, vol. VII., 4th series,
p. 219.) Dr Sanday (Hastings' *Bib. Dict.*, II. p. 634) definitely
abandons this way of explaining the discrepancy, and inclines to
the ancient theory of a transcriptional error, $F = 6$ being read for
$\Gamma = 3$ (*digamma* for *gamma*).

This is more satisfactory than a third explanation which rests
on the Oriental vagueness in regard to time. Professor Ramsay
remarks, 'To the Oriental mind the question between the third
hour and the sixth is not more important than the doubt between
12.5 and 12.10 P.M. is to us' (*loc. cit.* above). We cannot think
however that such vagueness is applicable to St John.

15.   Shall I crucify your King? Pilate was wholly impressed
with the Person of Jesus. For him the question was altogether
serious.

We have no king but Cæsar. No words could convey more
vividly the length to which their passion had carried the enemies

16 b–37.　The Crucifixion of Jesus.　Matt. xxvii. 32–56;
Mk xv. 21–41; Lk. xxiii. 26–49.

They took Jesus therefore: and he went out, bearing 17
the cross for himself, unto the place called The place of a
skull, which is called in Hebrew Golgotha: where they 18
crucified him, and with him two others, on either side one,
and Jesus in the midst.　And Pilate wrote a title also, 19
and put it on the cross.　And there was written, JESUS
OF NAZARETH, THE KING OF THE JEWS.　This title there- 20
fore read many of the Jews: for the place where Jesus

---

of Christ.　It was the abandonment of the national hope of a
Messiah king.

16.　At length the judicial sentence is given: the formula was,
Ibis ad crucem, 'Thou shalt go to the cross.'

17.　The place of a skull…Golgotha.　'The place which
is called the skull,' Lk. xxiv. 33.　The name is probably
derived from the skull-like shape of the hill.　But this is uncertain.　The site is also uncertain to this day.　The dispute is
between (1) the traditional site now covered by the Church of
the Holy Sepulchre and (2) a green round-topped hill near the
Damascus gate.　The question may perhaps be solved by dis-
covering the line of the city wall as it existed in our Saviour's
time.　The best authorities at the present time lean to the
traditional site.

18.　they, i.e. the Jews, as in Acts ii. 23; the crime is laid upon
the Jews, although the Roman soldiers were the actual doers of
it.　Thus Jew and Gentile joined in accomplishing 'the deter-
minate counsel' of God.

crucified him, a death both of terrible suffering, and also
of great ignominy.　No Roman citizen could be crucified.　The
death was reserved for slaves and criminals.　See Phil. ii. 8.

19.　wrote a title also.　It was usual to place a *titulus* or
placard on the cross, stating the crime for which the victim
suffered.　In this case the pains which Pilate took himself to
write the title, and that in three languages, and his persistence
in retaining it, 'What I have written, I have written' (*v.* 22),
are further proof of the deep impression made upon him by the
words and personality of Jesus.

20.　therefore, better than the ambiguous 'then,' A.V.　For
this mistranslation or omission of 'therefore,' see *vv.* 10 and 15.
By his frequent use of this word St John indicates the result or
effect of one act on another.　Here the fact that **many** read the
title follows from the nearness of the Cross to Jerusalem, and
the tri-lingual writing.

was crucified was nigh to the city: and it was written in
21 Hebrew, *and* in Latin, *and* in Greek. The chief priests
of the Jews therefore said to Pilate, Write not, The King
of the Jews; but, that he said, I am King of the Jews.
22 Pilate answered, What I have written I have written.

23   The soldiers therefore, when they had crucified Jesus,
took his garments, and made four parts, to every soldier
a part; and also the coat: now the coat was without
24 seam, woven from the top throughout. They said therefore one to another, Let us not rend it, but cast lots
for it, whose it shall be. that the scripture might be
fulfilled, which saith,

They parted my garments among them,
And upon my vesture did they cast lots.

25 These things therefore the soldiers did. But there were
standing by the cross of Jesus his mother, and his
mother's sister, Mary the *wife* of Clopas, and Mary

---

nigh to the city, therefore outside the walls. St John alone
mentions this fact. For the significance of it see Hebr. xiii.
11 foll.

23. garments, including the upper garment,—a large, square,
woollen robe,—the headdress, cincture or belt, and sandals.

to every soldier a part. The guard consisted of four
soldiers, a quaternion. Comp. Acts xii. 4. For greater security
Peter was placed in charge of four quaternions of soldiers.

coat, the under garment or tunic, which had sleeves and
reached below the knees.

24. They parted my garments...cast lots. See Ps. xxii. 18,
the last indignity for the crucified.

St John does not mention the darkness which fell upon the
scene and veiled the Saviour's dying agonies from human eyes
(Matt. xxvii. 45, and parallels). A darkness, which, it has been
well noted, should have precluded the crude representation of
Christ upon the Cross.

25. there were standing, &c. In all probability four women
are meant, for it is most unlikely that the Virgin Mary had a
sister of the same name. The unnamed woman may have been,
and probably was, St John's mother, Salome, the wife of Zebedee.
Mary the [wife] **of Clopas** or Cleopas. This Clopas is said by
Hegesippus (Euseb. *H. E.* III. 11) to have been the brother of
Joseph, the reputed father of our Lord. In Mark (xv. 40) Mary
is said to be mother of James the little and of Joses. The iden-

Magdalene. When Jesus therefore saw his mother, and 26 the disciple standing by, whom he loved, he saith unto his mother, Woman, behold, thy son! Then saith he to 27 the disciple, Behold, thy mother! And from that hour the disciple took her unto his own *home*.

After this Jesus, knowing that all things are now 28 finished, that the scripture might be accomplished, saith, I thirst. There was set there a vessel full of vinegar: so they 29 put a sponge full of the vinegar upon hyssop, and brought it to his mouth. When Jesus therefore had received the 30 vinegar, he said, It is finished. and he bowed his head, and gave up his spirit.

---

tification of Alphæus with Clopas is not permissible, but it is possible that this Mary was the daughter of Clopas and the wife of Alphæus.

In Luke we read that the women from Galilee 'stood afar off,' but St John speaks as an eye-witness. It would appear that he alone of the Apostles remained at the Cross.

26 the disciple...whom he loved. See ch. xiii. 23. By these words from the Cross Jesus brought together the two whom, humanly, He loved best in the world. 'The brethren of the Lord,' the natural protectors of Mary, still did not believe on Jesus as the Christ. In a deeper sense St John was His brother (Matt. xii. 49). And, if Salome was sister to the Virgin Mary, he was more truly a kinsman than 'the brethren of the Lord.'

28. that the scripture might be accomplished, Ps. lxix. 21. These notes of St John on the Saviour's secret thoughts are deeply interesting. They are the result of the beloved disciple's intimate knowledge of the mind of Christ (1 Cor. ii. 16).

I thirst, the final, and perhaps the most agonising, pain of crucifixion. This is the fifth word from the Cross.

29. they put a sponge full of the vinegar upon hyssop. This draught intended to quench the thirst must be distinguished from 'the wine mingled with gall' (Matt.) or 'with myrrh' (Mk) given to deaden pain, which Jesus refused to take (Matt. xxvii. 34) lest the clearness of His intelligence should suffer.

The **vinegar** is the soldier's sour wine or *posca*. **Hyssop**, probably the caper (*capparis spinosa*), which still grows on the walls of Jerusalem and on the rocks in the Kidron valley (Tristram, *Nat. Hist. of the Bible*, p. 455 foll.). It has stems three or four feet long.

30. It is finished, the sixth word from the Cross—and one

31 The Jews therefore, because it was the Preparation, that
the bodies should not remain on the cross upon the
sabbath (for the day of that sabbath was a high *day*),
asked of Pilate that their legs might be broken, and *that*
32 they might be taken away. The soldiers therefore came,
and brake the legs of the first, and of the other which was
33 crucified with him: but when they came to Jesus, and
saw that he was dead already, they brake not his legs

34-37. Piercing of the side of Jesus, narrated by St John
alone: comp. 1 John v. 6-8.

34 howbeit one of the soldiers with a spear pierced his side,
35 and straightway there came out blood and water. And

---

full of the deepest significance. The work of redemption in all
its fulness was accomplished.

gave up his spirit, for 'gave up the ghost,' A.V The Greek
implies the free transmission or rendering of His spirit to God,
the willing offering of His soul (see ch. x. 18). It is St John's
reference to the last word from the Cross recorded by St Luke
alone : 'Father, into thy hands I commend my spirit' (Luke
xxiii. 46).

31. the Preparation. See *v.* 14.

that the bodies...upon the sabbath. See Deut. xxi. 23,
where the reason is given.

that sabbath was a high day, being the day at the commencement of which the Passover was celebrated, viz. Nisan 15. At
that moment the paschal lambs were being sacrificed in the
Temple courts.

32. brake the legs. This was done in order to assure the
death of the sufferer.

34. pierced, a different word in the Greek from that used in
v. 37. Dr Field suggests 'pricked.' The act was done, not out
of wanton cruelty, but to ascertain if He were dead.

there came out blood and water. The profound significance of this fact in relation to the two sacraments is noted,
1 John v. 6, 8. Observe there the careful rendering of the R.V.
Bishop Westcott notes that 'Blood is the symbol of the natural
life, and so especially of the life sacrificed': comp. chs. i. 13 and
vi. 53-56, and Rev. i. 5, v. 9, vii. 14 ; '...and water the symbol
of spiritual life': comp. chs. iii. 5, iv. 14, vii. 38. The cleansing
from sin, and the quickening by the Spirit, are both consequent
on Christ's death.

he that hath seen hath borne witness, and his witness is
true : and he knoweth that he saith true, that ye also may
believe. For these things came to pass, that the scripture 36
might be fulfilled, A bone of him shall not be broken.
And again another scripture saith, They shall look on him 37
whom they pierced.

38–42. The Burial of Jesus, Matt. xxvii. 57–61 ; Mk xv.
    42–47 ; Lk. xxiii. 50–56.

And after these things Joseph of Arimathæa, being a 38
disciple of Jesus, but secretly for fear of the Jews, asked
of Pilate that he might take away the body of Jesus : and
Pilate gave *him* leave. He came therefore, and took
away his body. And there came also Nicodemus, he who 39
at the first came to him by night, bringing a mixture of

---

35. he that hath seen. The reference is to St John himself.
The use of the third person is quite in accordance with the
Evangelist's practice. Comp. Matt. ix. 9, where St Matthew
speaks of himself as a third person.

true...true. Different words are used in the Greek. Together they imply the authority of the witness, and the exactness
of his evidence.

36, 37. This is a reflexion by St John long after the event :
who sees in it a fulfilment of prophecy. See (*a*) Exod. xii. 46 ;
Ps. xxxiv. 20 ; (*b*) Zech. xii. 10 ; comp. Rev. i. 7.

As Bp Westcott notes, these quotations are not exhaustive.
They indicate the 'two great lines of preparatory teaching.'

38. Joseph, a member of the Sanhedrin, who however 'had
not consented to their counsel and deed ' and 'who was looking
for the Kingdom of God,' Luke xxiii..51 ; Mk xv. 43.

Arimathæa, sometimes identified with Ramathaim Zophim,
but its position is at present unknown.

Pilate gave him leave. Another sign of Pilate's conviction
of the innocence of Jesus. If he had believed the charge of
treason, no indignity would have been spared. This was an
act of some courage on the part of Pilate, and one of great
courage on the part of Joseph and Nicodemus to give honour-
able burial to One against whom the popular hatred raged so
fiercely.

39. he who...by night. A note, which shews the unity of
authorship, and integrity of this Gospel.

a mixture, *marg.* a roll.

40 myrrh and aloes, about a hundred pound *weight*. So
they took the body of Jesus, and bound it in linen cloths
with the spices, as the custom of the Jews is to bury.
41 Now in the place where he was crucified there was a
garden; and in the garden a new tomb wherein was
42 never man yet laid. There then because of the Jews'
Preparation (for the tomb was nigh at hand) they laid
Jesus.

> 20 1-18. The visit of Mary Magdalene, and of St Peter and
> St John, to the tomb, 1-10.

20   Now on the first *day* of the week cometh Mary Magdalene early, while it was yet dark, unto the tomb, and
2 seeth the stone taken away from the tomb. She runneth
therefore, and cometh to Simon Peter, and to the other
disciple, whom Jesus loved, and saith unto them, They
have taken away the Lord out of the tomb, and we know
3 not where they have laid him. Peter therefore went
forth, and the other disciple, and they went toward the
4 tomb.   And they ran both together: and the other

---

about a hundred pound weight. A princely gift. The spices
would be massed around and over the body. See 2 Chr. xvi. 14.
41. a new tomb, hewn out of the rock, and closed at the
entrance by a circular stone (*golal*) which was rolled in a channel
or groove. St Matthew notes that it belonged to Joseph
(xxvii. 60).
the tomb was nigh at hand. There was need of haste, **as**
the Feast commenced at sunset.

XX. 1. Mary Magdalene, 'and the other Mary' (Matt.), 'and
Mary, the mother of James, and Salome' (Mk), 'the women
which came with him from Galilee' (Luke). Probably Mary
Magdalene alone went to inform St Peter and St John; though
according to the synoptic accounts the *women* told the Apostles,
but it is to be remembered that there were several Apostles, who
may have been in different places.
the first day of the week...early, i.e. early on Sunday
morning; for though the Jewish day technically began at sunset,
morning and evening meant as with us the beginning and end of
the natural day.
taken away, lit. 'lifted out of.' The synoptists speak of the
stone as being 'rolled away.'

disciple outran Peter, and came first to the tomb; and 5
stooping and looking in, he seeth the linen cloths lying;
yet entered he not in. Simon Peter therefore also cometh, 6
following him, and entered into the tomb; and he beholdeth the linen cloths lying, and the napkin, that was upon 7
his head, not lying with the linen cloths, but rolled up in
a place by itself. Then entered in therefore the other 8
disciple also, which came first to the tomb, and he saw,
and believed. For as yet they knew not the scripture, 9
that he must rise again from the dead. So the disciples 10
went away again unto their own home.

11-18. The appearance to Mary Magdalene.

But Mary was standing without at the tomb weeping: 11

---

4. outran Peter, as being the younger man.

5. stooping and looking in, or perhaps looking *down*. The
verb is thus used in a recently discovered *papyrus* (see *Expositor*,
Dec. 1903, p. 437). The phrase is expressed by one word in
the Greek.

seeth but does not closely observe. It was still dark.

6. beholdeth, i.e. sees and observes carefully. What he
saw was the linen swathing bands undisturbed, but fallen flat
through the absence of the body, the napkin, which had been
around the head, twisted round or 'rolled up' was detached
from the other grave-clothes and perhaps rested on a stone which
had served as a pillow.

8. he saw. A different word from that used *v.* 5, it is connected with the word 'to know.' From that moment was dated
St John's knowledge of the Resurrection. No other inference
was possible from the facts observed. Of St Peter it is said,
'he departed to his home, wondering at that which was come to
pass,' Luke xxiv. 12.

9. they knew not the scripture. See Acts ii. 25-31, where
Ps. xvi. 10, probably the definite 'scripture' referred to here, is
cited. Comp. Luke xxiv. 26, 45.

The note is important as shewing that the Resurrection was
not a preconceived notion on the part of the Apostles. It was
an event for which they were unprepared.

11. But Mary, &c. Mary though unmentioned in the narrative
had been with the Apostles, and remained when they returned
home.

weeping. Not silently, as Jesus wept at the tomb of
Lazarus, but weeping aloud.

so, as she wept, she stooped and looked into the tomb;
12 and she beholdeth two angels in white sitting, one at the
head, and one at the feet, where the body of Jesus had
13 lain. And they say unto her, Woman, why weepest
thou? She saith unto them, Because they have taken
away my Lord, and I know not where they have laid him.
14 When she had thus said, she turned herself back, and
beholdeth Jesus standing, and knew not that it was Jesus.
15 Jesus saith unto her, Woman, why weepest thou? whom
seekest thou? She, supposing him to be the gardener,
saith unto him, Sir, if thou hast borne him hence, tell me
where thou hast laid him, and I will take him away.
16 Jesus saith unto her, Mary. She turneth herself, and
saith unto him in Hebrew, Rabboni; which is to say,
17 Master. Jesus saith to her, Touch me not; for I am not

---

13. Because...laid him. See *v.* 2.

14. knew not that it was Jesus. Comp. Mk xvi. 12 and
Luke xxiv. 16. The identity of Jesus was unaltered, but some
change had passed over the body, which rendered it not
immediately recognisable.

16. Mary. The Greek retains the Hebrew (Aramaic) form,
Mariam. She recognised the familiar form of the name, and
the familiar tone of voice, and answered in the same dialect.

17. Touch me not, better as *marg.* take not hold on me, or
more accurately, 'do not continue to cling to me.' The act is
explained by St Matthew's report of the appearance of Jesus to
the women returning from the sepulchre : 'And they came and
took hold of his feet and worshipped him' (Matt. xxviii. 9).
The action of Mary was probably one to which she was used in
days past. She thought perhaps that the Master's renewed
presence was to be continuous. Our Lord's words point to
a further change. The former conditions have passed; and yet
the new conditions have not been perfected. The present-
perfect, 'I am not yet ascended,' and still more the present,
'I am ascending unto my Father,' imply that the spiritual change
which ended in the Ascension had begun and was in progress.
Hence the object of Christian worship is the ascended Christ.
St Paul has taught that the object of Christian love and worship
is 'the Lord Jesus Christ in incorruptibility' (ἐν ἀφθαρσίᾳ), Eph.
vi. 24, i.e. in His glorified state after the Ascension. This
interval between the Resurrection and Ascension was neither

yet ascended unto the Father: but go unto my brethren,
and say to them, I ascend unto my Father and your
Father, and my God and your God.   Mary Magdalene 18
cometh and telleth the disciples, I have seen the Lord;
and *how that* he had said these things unto her.

19–23. The appearance to ten of the Apostles and others,
Mk xvi. 14; Lk. xxiv. 36–43. St Mark adds 'as they sat
at meat'; St Luke says, 'they were terrified and affrighted.'
The definite details are peculiar to this Gospel.

When therefore it was evening, on that day, the first 19
day of the week, and when the doors were shut where the
disciples were, for fear of the Jews, Jesus came and stood
in the midst, and saith unto them, Peace *be* unto you.
And when he had said this, he shewed unto them his 20
hands and his side. The disciples therefore were glad,
when they saw the Lord. Jesus therefore said to them 21
again, Peace *be* unto you: as the Father hath sent me,
even so send I you. And when he had said this, he 22

---

appropriate to the old relations of friendship, nor to the future
condition of adoration.

my brethren. See Hebr. ii. 11. Only after the Resurrection
does Jesus call His disciples brethren. Now that the Lord had
risen there was the more need to remind them that the human
nature remained. He was still the 'Son of Man.'

19. where the disciples were. Many no doubt were
gathered on hearing rumours of the Resurrection.

Peace be unto you. Jesus gives a fresh significance to the
ordinary salutation. It is 'a peace that passeth understanding.'

19, 20. These two verses indicate the conditions of the body
of the risen Lord. It is spiritual and immaterial, and yet it
exhibits the marks and proofs of crucifixion. It differs both
from the body which He wore on earth, and also from that which
He wears in heaven. It was adapted to the unique conditions
which existed in that unparalleled period of time between the
Resurrection and the Ascension. Its properties are partly
spiritual, partly material.

21. even so send I you. This is the foundation of the
Apostolate. Hitherto the mission had been confined to Galilee.
It is now extended to all the world—to every creature (Matt.
xxviii. 20), and its range defined, Acts i. 8. The word used for

breathed on them, and saith unto them, Receive ye the
23 Holy Ghost. whose soever sins ye forgive, they are
forgiven unto them; whose soever *sins* ye retain, they
are retained.

24, 25.   The doubting of Thomas.

24   But Thomas, one of the twelve, called Didymus, was
25 not with them when Jesus came.   The other disciples
therefore said unto him, We have seen the Lord.   But he
said unto them, Except I shall see in his hands the print
of the nails, and put my finger into the print of the nails,
and put my hand into his side, I will not believe.

---

the mission of the Son by the Father is different from that used
of the mission of the Apostles; which is a word applicable to
the sending forth of ambassadors; comp. 'We are ambassadors
on behalf of Christ,' 2 Cor. v. 20.

22.   breathed on them.   A sign of the new life, comp. Gen.
ii. 7.   'The Lord God breathed into his nostrils the breath of
life.'   So here also breath is the symbol of the new life, and the
means by which it was conferred.   Both in Hebrew (**ruach**) and
in Greek (**pneuma**), the same words are used for 'breath' and
'spirit.'

23.   whose soever sins ye forgive, &c.   These words were
addressed to the ten Apostles (Thomas being absent) and to
others with them.   See Luke xxiv. 33.   The privilege therefore
is conferred on the Church, the whole community of the followers
of Christ.   For the meaning of the expression comp. Matt. xvi.
19, where authority to 'bind' and 'loose,' i.e. to forbid or to
allow, to declare a sin forgiven or still unforgiven, is conferred on
St Peter, who thus became 'a scribe of the kingdom of heaven.'
For the same words were used in the appointment of a Jewish
scribe.   As in other instances the existing custom was used; but
invested with a deeper meaning by Christ.

The tenses, 'are forgiven,' 'are retained,' should be noted.
The sins which you, through the Holy Ghost, pronounce to be
forgiven, have already been forgiven in heaven.   Spiritual
insight discerns the mind of Christ.

24.   called Didymus, i.e. Twin;   Thomas has the same
meaning.

one of the twelve, the name still remains notwithstanding
the defection of Judas; see 1 Cor. xv. 5.

25.   The character of incredulity is strongly marked by the
definiteness and force of these expressions.   He had abandoned
all hope; no mere verbal evidence would convince him.

26-29.   The doubts of Thomas removed.

And after eight days again his disciples were within, 26
and Thomas with them.   Jesus cometh, the doors being
shut, and stood in the midst, and said, Peace *be* unto you.
Then saith he to Thomas, Reach hither thy finger, and 27
see my hands; and reach *hither* thy hand, and put
it into my side: and be not faithless, but believing.
Thomas answered and said unto him, My Lord and my 28
God.   Jesus saith unto him, Because thou hast seen me, 29
thou hast believed: blessed *are* they that have not seen,
and *yet* have believed.

30-31.   The purpose of the Evangelist in writing the Gospel.

Many other signs therefore did Jesus in the presence 30
of the disciples, which are not written in this book: but 31
these are written, that ye may believe that Jesus is the

---

27. be not faithless, lit. do not *become* faithless, let your
growth be in faith not in incredulity.

28. My Lord and my God.   A declaration of faith far exceeding any yet uttered by any disciple of Jesus.   Strength of
incredulity had given place to strength of faith.   Still we must
note that our Lord gives no commendation to St Thomas, as He
did to St Peter when he made his confession of the Godhead of
Christ, Matt. xvi. 17.   The blessing here is to those who believe
on the testimony of others (*v.* 29).   As Godet notes, the words
form a fitting transition from the Gospel to the Acts.

30. Many other signs.   The reference is to the whole of the
Gospel narrative, and not only to the history of the forty days,
as some have thought.   St John records eight miracles only
(including ch. xxi.) and no instances of healing lepers or possessed persons.   But in naming the 'other signs' he bears
witness to the truth of them.

in this book, as distinct from other books or Gospels in which
they are written.

31. these are written......life in his name.   A deeply
important declaration of the aim of the Gospel: (*a*) belief in
Jesus as the Christ, the Son of God: (*b*) the gift of life which
that belief confers.   The same belief, and the same purpose, are
stated in the prologue.   'The Word was God...and the Word
became flesh' (ch. i. 1, 14).   'In him was life, and the life was
the light of men' (ch. i. 4).   Throughout the Gospel this aim is
consistently kept in view.   The words and works of Christ are

Christ, the Son of God; and that believing ye may have
life in his name.

21 1-14. A Manifestation of Jesus to seven Disciples at the
Sea of Tiberias.

21 After these things Jesus manifested himself again to
the disciples at the sea of Tiberias; and he manifested
2 *himself* on this wise. There were together Simon Peter,
and Thomas called Didymus, and Nathanael of Cana in

---

presented as the words and works of God. Comp. with the
whole thought of the verse 1 John iv. 15, 'Whosoever shall
confess that Jesus is the Son of God, God abideth in him,
and he in God'; and v. 11–13.

Son of God. To the Oriental mind this expression would
convey no idea of inferiority, but of identity with God in nature
and being.

With this verse the Gospel of St John undoubtedly ends as
originally planned. It ends as it began with a declaration of
the Divine nature of the Christ. St Thomas stands forth as
representative of the central truth of this Gospel, and of the
Christian faith.

Chapter xxi. is an appendix, added probably at some earnest
request of St John's disciples desiring further knowledge of
what passed in the great forty days.

The style of ch. xxi. is essentially Johannine. The same
words and connecting particles are used. There is the same love
of accurate detail which is observable elsewhere. The description
of persons too is characteristic of St John.

All the MSS. contain the chapter. It may even have been
written a few days only after the Gospel was finished, and before
it was published.

XXI. 1. manifested himself, more significant than 'shewed
himself' A.V.

sea of Tiberias. See ch. vi. 1. Both the Hebrew and
Greek words for 'sea' are used of a vast expanse of water like
the Mediterranean Sea, as well as for small lakes or pools as
the Salt or Dead Sea, and the 'sea of Jazer' (Jer. xlviii. 32).

Tiberias, a city built by Herod Antipas, and not named in
the synoptics. It was destroyed by Vespasian, but was rebuilt
and became the seat of a famous Rabbinical School.

2. Nathanael. The way in which this disciple is mentioned
leads to the inference that he was one of the Twelve, and that
the theory which identifies him with Bartholomew is right.

Galilee and the *sons* of Zebedee, and two other of his
disciples Simon Peter saith unto them, I go a fishing. 3
They say unto him, We also come with thee. They
went forth, and entered into the boat; and that night
they took nothing. But when day was now break- 4
ing, Jesus stood on the beach: howbeit the disciples
knew not that it was Jesus. Jesus therefore saith unto 5
them, Children, have ye aught to eat? They answered
him, No. And he said unto them, Cast the net on the 6
right side of the boat, and ye shall find. They cast
therefore, and now they were not able to draw it for the
multitude of fishes. That disciple therefore whom Jesus 7
loved saith unto Peter, It is the Lord. So when Simon
Peter heard that it was the Lord, he girt his coat about
him (for he was naked), and cast himself into the sea.

---

the sons of Zebedee. The only passage in which St John and
his brother James are thus named together in this Gospel.

3. the boat, for 'a ship,' A.V.

that night, the favourable time for fishing.

4. when day was now breaking, an improvement on,
'when the morning was now come,' A.V. The dimness of the
early dawn perhaps accounted for the failure to recognise Jesus.
Also from ch. xx. 14 it appears that some indefinable change had
passed over our Lord's risen and glorified Body.

This manifestation of Jesus was in fulfilment of the promise
that He would 'go before them,' as the Shepherd of His
beloved flock, 'into Galilee.' Matt. xxvi. 32.

5. Children, or rather 'boys' (Greek, *paidia*, not the affectionate *teknia*, as xiii. 33), a term that might be used even by
a stranger to the fishermen. The disciples were still some
distance from the shore, and the voice may have sounded as of
one asking whether they had any food for sale: 'have you
caught anything?' See Stanley, *Sinai and Palestine*, p. 378.

6. Cast the net...ye shall find. The direction is followed,
though Jesus is still not recognised.

7. It is from this passage that we are enabled with certainty
to identify 'the disciple whom Jesus loved' with St John.

for he was naked, he had thrown off his outer garment,
having only his tunic: comp. the Virgilian direction to the
husbandman, 'Nudus ara, sere nudus.' Possibly however Peter
was naked with the exception of a loin-cloth.

This 'sign' must be compared with the other miraculous

8 But the other disciples came in the little boat (for they
were not far from the land, but about two hundred cubits
9 off), dragging the net *full* of fishes. So when they got out
upon the land, they see a fire of coals there, and fish laid
10 thereon, and bread. Jesus saith unto them, Bring of the
11 fish which ye have now taken. Simon Peter therefore
went up, and drew the net to land, full of great fishes, a
hundred and fifty and three: and for all there were so
12 many, the net was not rent. Jesus saith unto them, Come
and break your fast. And none of the disciples durst
inquire of him, Who art thou? knowing that it was the
13 Lord. Jesus cometh, and taketh the bread, and giveth
14 them, and the fish likewise. This is now the third time
that Jesus was manifested to the disciples, after that he
was risen from the dead.

15-19. The charge to St Peter.

15   So when they had broken their fast, Jesus saith to Simon

---

draught of fishes, when at least two of those now present were
called to be fishers of men. The circumstances differ in many
respects. Luke v. 5 *foll.*

8. the little boat, the small boat, as distinct from the larger
fishing boat.

9. they see a fire...and bread. According to Chrysostom
and others the fire of coals and the bread and the fish were
miraculously provided. But this inference is not necessary; for
the Apostles or their servants may have made provision for
a meal when the night's toil was over.

11. went up, *marg.* 'aboard.' The miracle is no doubt
symbolic (Luke v. 10), but some have pressed the imagery too
far, seeing for instance in the number 153 the exact number of
the races of men to whom the Gospel has been preached. Dean
Colet turned the number to beautiful account in his foundation
for 153 scholars in St Paul's School.

12. break your fast, an improvement on 'dine,' A.V. See
also *v.* 15.

13. taketh the bread......and the fish likewise. This act
must have recalled the miracle of feeding the 5000, ch. vi. 23.

14. the third time, i.e. the third time to the Apostles in
a body. The separate appearances to Mary Magdalene and the
other women and to the two disciples on the way to Emmaus
are not taken into account.

Peter, Simon, *son* of John, lovest thou me more than
these? He saith unto him, Yea, Lord; thou knowest that
I love thee. He saith unto him, Feed my lambs. He 16
saith to him again a second time, Simon, *son* of John,
lovest thou me? He saith unto him, Yea, Lord; thou
knowest that I love thee. He saith unto him, Tend my
sheep. He saith unto him the third time, Simon, *son* of 17
John, lovest thou me? Peter was grieved because he said
unto him the third time, Lovest thou me? And he said
unto him, Lord, thou knowest all things; thou knowest
that I love thee. Jesus saith unto him, Feed my sheep.
Verily, verily, I say unto thee, When thou wast young, 18
thou girdedst thyself, and walkedst whither thou wouldest:
but when thou shalt be old, thou shalt stretch forth thy

---

15. Simon, son of John, for 'Simon son of Jonas,' A.V.

lovest thou me...thou knowest that I love thee. Different
Greek words are used in our Lord's question and in St Peter's
answer. In the third question however our Lord uses St Peter's
word. The word which Jesus uses expresses a full and complete
love (*agapè*) ; St Peter's word, used in humility, is that of ordinary
friendship (*philia*). The three professions of love have relation
to the three denials of St Peter. The confession is threefold, as
the sin was threefold.

Feed my lambs. 'Feed' implies individual care in giving
spiritual nourishment ; the *lambs*, perhaps not only the children of
Christ's flock, but also, weaker disciples who need special care.

16. Tend (for 'feed,' A.V.) **my sheep.** Be a shepherd to my
flock. To tend is more than to feed; it implies direction and
government.

17. thou knowest that I love thee. An appeal to the
Divine intuition of Jesus. Comp. Acts i. 24, xv. 8, where a
compound word confined in its use to St Peter expresses this
Divine knowledge of human hearts.

Feed my sheep, the elder members of the Church of Christ
also need individual care and nutriment. The triple charge may
be paraphrased : 'Take thought for individual souls of young
and old alike, and guide and rule the Church of Christ.' The
interpretation of these words lies in history. That no autocratic
power was intended is shewn by St Paul's rebuke to St Peter at
Antioch (Gal. ii. 11), and by St Peter's defence of his conduct
before the assembled disciples in Jerusalem (Acts xi. 4 *foll.*).

18. when thou shalt be old. St Peter suffered death in A.D.

hands, and another shall gird thee, and carry thee whither
19 thou wouldest not. Now this he spake, signifying by
what manner of death he should glorify God. And when
he had spoken this, he saith unto him, Follow me.

20–23. The words of Jesus about St John misinterpreted.

20 Peter, turning about, seeth the disciple whom Jesus loved
following; which also leaned back on his breast at the
supper, and said, Lord, who is he that betrayeth thee?
21 Peter therefore seeing him saith to Jesus, Lord, and what
22 shall this man do? Jesus saith unto him, If I will that he
tarry till I come, what *is that* to thee? follow thou me.

---

64 ; according to Origen he was crucified head downwards at his
own request. (Eus. *H. E.* III. I.)

shalt stretch forth thy hands, not, as some have thought,
upon the cross, but for assistance.

19. this he spake, &c. St John, as often in this Gospel,
interprets the meaning of the words of Jesus.

by what manner of death, for 'by what death,' A.V.
Our Lord predicts a death of martyrdom, not the precise form
of crucifixion.

Follow me. See ch. xiii. 37. 'Lord, why cannot I follow
thee even now?' St Peter now understands why he could not
then follow Christ. He needed the bitter experience of failure,
and the lesson of humility. The repeated 'follow me' of Christ
with clear reference to the past signified the need of this discipline
and the blessing of it.

But 'Follow me' has also reference to the future. Peter was
to follow Christ to the Cross. The words recall the expression,
'Take up thy cross and follow me.'

20. Peter, turning about, &c. St Peter, at the command of
Jesus, follows Him to receive, it may be, some direction apart
from the other disciples, or perhaps some more express word of
pardon. He turned round and saw St John following. The
phrase by which St John describes himself implies the claim, as
the beloved disciple, to join Jesus and St Peter.

21. and what shall this man do? Jesus had foretold what
would happen to St Peter. It was natural for St Peter to
enquire what fate was destined for his friend.

22. Jesus saith...what is that to thee? Jesus as at other
times declines to give a direct prediction (comp. Matt. xxiv. 3,
36 ; Acts i. 7).

till I come. As St John himself explains, Jesus does not

This saying therefore went forth among the brethren, that 23
that disciple should not die: yet Jesus said not unto him,
that he should not die; but, If I will that he tarry till I
come, what *is that* to thee?

This is the disciple which beareth witness of these 24
things, and wrote these things: and we know that his
witness is true.

And there are also many other things which Jesus did, 25
the which if they should be written every one, I suppose
that even the world itself would not contain the books that
should be written.

---

promise or predict that John should survive until His second
coming, but that his life and the ending of it rested with God.

24, 25.   A note added probably by the disciples of St John
affirming the truth of the Gospel as delivered by their master.
It has relation not alone to chapter xxi. but to all that has
preceded.

24.   we know, i.e. we, his disciples and the whole Church,
know; below *v.* 25 the disciple speaks in his own name, 'I
suppose.'

25.   even the world itself...should be written.   This hyper-
bole expresses the writer's intense conviction of the grandeur and
inexhaustible significance of all that Jesus did.

INDEX.

Abiding in Christ, 42, 100
Abraham, 56, 58
Adultery, woman taken in, 50
Alogi, the, xi
Andrew, 8, 36, 83
Annas, 115, 116
Arrest of Jesus, 114
Ass, a symbol of peace, 81

Bag or box for money, 79, 91
Baptism, of John, 5 ; alluded
  to, 15, 89
Barabbas, 119
Believe, to, and to believe *on*,
  54
Benson, Dr, quoted, xiv, 121
Bethany, on the Jordan, 6 ;
  near Jerusalem, 78
Bethesda, 28
Bethsaida, 9
Betrayal of Jesus ; *see* Arrest
Blind from birth, man, 59
Blood and water, meaning of,
  126
Blood of Christ, 41
Body of the Lord after Resur-
  rection, 131
Bondage, 55
Bread of Life, the, 39, 40
Brethren of the Lord, 44
Brethren, disciples so called,
  131

Caiaphas, 76
Call of the disciples, the first,
  8
Cana of Galilee, 10, 26, 134
Capernaum, 12, 37, 42
Catacombs, evidence from, xi
Cephas, 9 ; *see* Peter
Church, the, foreshadowed, 64
Cleansing of the Temple, 13
Clement of Alexandria, x
Comforter, the, 14, 96, 98
Commandment, the new, 92

Dedication, Feast of the, 68
Deity of Christ, 70
Denarius ; see Penny
Devil, *diabolus*, 43, 56 ; *dai-
  monion*, 46, 68
Disciple, the, whom Jesus
  loved, xiii, 90, 125, 128, 138
Disciples of John, 8, 18
Discourses in this Gospel, xxv,
  foll.
Dispersion, the, 47
Draught of fishes, 135
Drummond, Dr James, quoted,
  xiv

Ebal, 23
Elijah, 5
Ephesus, x
Ephraim, 77

Equality of Christ with the
	Father, 30
Eternal life, 31, 39, 41, 87,
	109
Exodus quoted, 127

Feast of Trumpets, 27, 28; of
	Tabernacles, 44; of The
	Dedication, 68; *see* Passover
Flesh, the, of Christ, 41
Forgiveness of sins, 132
Freedom, 55

Galilee, 44, 50
Garden (Gethsemane), 113
Garments, 124
Genesis quoted, 10
Gentiles, the, 67, 77, 82
Gerizim, 23
Glorified, meaning of, 48, 83,
	91, 109
Glory, the, of God, 59, 72
Golgotha, 123
Gospel, the Fourth, its object
	and characteristics, xviii
Grace, 3
Greeks, 82

Hallel, the, 81
Holy one of God, 43
Hosanna, 81

Irenæus, ix
Isaiah quoted, 5, 40, 85, 86
Iscariot, Simon, 43; Judas, 43,
	79, 88, 91, 113

Jacob's vision, 10
Jerusalem, 5, 13, 23, 26, 27,
	68, 73, 78, 81
John the son of Zebedee,
	author of this Gospel, ix;
	life of, xv, 8, 125, 138.
	See also 'Disciple whom
	Jesus loved'
John the Baptist, 2, 4, 6, 8,
	18, 20, 32
Joseph of Arimathæa, 127

Joy, 101, 107
Judæa, the Lord's own country,
	26
Judas Iscariot; *see* Iscariot
Judas Lebbæus, 97
Judgement, 105
Judgement seat, 121

Kelvin, Lord, on creation, 1
Kidron, the, 112
King of the Jews, 118

Lamb of God, the, 6
Lamp, the, that burneth and
	shineth, 32
Last Supper, the, 88, 93
Lazarus, 71
Life, 2, 41, 95, 133
'Lifting up, the,' of Christ,
	54, 84
Light, 2, 17, 85; Christ the
	Light of the world, 51, 60, 87
Lodge, Sir O., on creation, 1
Logos, the, or the Word, xxi,
	1, 3, 63, 95
Love, different words for, 137

Malchus, 114
Mansions, 94
Marriage in Cana, 11
Martha, 71
Martyr, the first, 63
Mary the mother of our Lord,
	11, 12, 124
Mary of Bethany, 71
Mary the *wife* of Clopas, 124
Mary Magdalene, 124, 128, 129
Maundy Thursday, meaning
	of, 92
Mission of the Apostles, 131
Muratorian Fragment, x

Naked, meaning of, 135
Napkin for the head, 75, 129
Nathanael, 9, 134
Nicodemus, 15, 49, 127
Nobleman, or king's officer,
	26

Notes by the Evangelist, 17, 82, 127

Ointment of spikenard, 79
Oneness of Christ with the Father, 29, 30, 52, 70, 95, 110
Origen, x

Passover, Feast of the, 12, 35, 77, 78, 93, 117, 119
Penny or *denarius*, meaning of, 35, 79
Persecution, 103
Peter, 8, 43, 88, 90, 92, 114, 115, 134, 137
Pharisees, 5, 20, 47, 52, 61, 64, 66, 76, 82, 86, 113
Philip, 9, 35, 82
Polycarp, a disciple of John, ix
Pontius Pilate, 117, 127
Prætorium, 117
Preparation of the Passover, 122, 126
Prince of the world, 99
Procurator, 117
Prophet, the, 5, 36, 48, 50
Proverbs, 107
Psalms quoted, 13, 39, 70, 81, 90, 102, 124, 125, 127
Purification, 11, 18, 78
Purple garment, 120

Rabbi, 8, 15
Recognition of God in Christ, 56
Resurrection power of Christ, 31, 73
Resurrection, effect of, on the Body of Christ, 131
Righteousness, 105
Romans, the, 76

Sabbath day, cures on, 28, 30, 61
Salome, xv
Samaria and Samaritans, 20, 25
Scourging, 119

Scriptures, their witness to Christ, 33
Self-sacrifice of Christ, 67
Sheepgate, 28
Shepherd, the good, 66
Signs or miracles, 16, 27, 38, 63, 85
Siloam, Pool of, 60
Simon Peter; *see* Peter
Simon the leper, 78
Sin, sometimes the cause of suffering, 29, 105
Sinlessness of Christ, 57
Sixth hour, the, 122
Solomon's Porch, 68
Son of God, 7, 121, 134
Son of Man, 16, 31, 85
Sychar, 21
Synagogue, expulsion from, 62, 103

Tatian's *Diatessaron*, xi
Temple, the, 13, 45, 52, 58
Thomas, 72, 132; his great confession, 133
Tiberias, 34; Sea of, 35, 134
Title on the Cross, 123
Tomb of Christ, 128
Towel, 88
Treasury of the Temple, 52
Trials of Jesus Christ, order of, 114
Truth, 3, 18, 45, 55, 95, 97, 119

Unity of the Church, 67, 111

Vine, 99
Vinegar, 125
Voice from heaven, 7, 84

Washing of the disciples' feet, 89
Water of life, 22
Way, the, 95
Witnesses for Christ, 32, 33, 52, 103

Women, customs in regard to, 24

Word, the; *see* Logos

Words from the Cross, 125

Work, creative, 29; the work of God, 38; greater works, 30, 96; works of Christ as witnessing to Him, 32

World, the, 102, 104, 118

Zebedee, sons of, 135

Zechariah quoted, 81, 127

For EU product safety concerns, contact us at Calle de José Abascal, 56–1°, 28003 Madrid, Spain or eugpsr@cambridge.org.

www.ingramcontent.com/pod-product-compliance
Ingram Content Group UK Ltd.
Pitfield, Milton Keynes, MK11 3LW, UK
UKHW020310140625
459647UK00018B/1821